The Redeeming Road

By A.B. DeBruyn

The Sheathed Quill Press
Houston, Texas

Copyright © 2023 Arthur B. DeBruyn

All rights reserved. No part of this book may be reproduced in any form or by any electronic or mechanical means, including information storage and retrieval systems, without permission in writing from the publisher, except by reviewers, who may quote brief passages in a review.

Scripture quotations marked MSG are taken from THE MESSAGE, copyright © 1993, 2002, 2018 by Eugene H. Peterson. Used by permission of NavPress. All rights reserved. Represented by Tyndale House Publishers, Inc.

Scripture quotations marked ERV are taken from the Easy-to-Read Version, copyright © 2006 by Bible League International.

Scripture quotations marked NIV are taken from the New International Version, THE HOLY BIBLE, NEW INTERNATIONAL VERSION®, NIV® Copyright © 1973, 1978, 1984, 2011 by Biblica, Inc.® Used by permission. All rights reserved worldwide.

ISBN (Kindle Edition)
ISBN (Paperback Edition) 978-0-9992445-1-7

Editing by Sean Guillemette
Cover image and interior line art based on images by Arthur B. DeBruyn
Book design by Sean Guillemette

Printed and bound in the USA
First Printing November 2023

Published by The Sheathed Quill Press
P.O. Box 5298
Kingwood, TX, USA 77325
Email: info@thesheathedquill.com

Visit www.thesheathedquill.com

Acknowledgements

The opportunity to write this devotional has been nothing short of a privilege. The list of who to acknowledge and thank for its successful publication began long before my fingers touched the keyboard. First and foremost, I give glory to God, who is the ultimate source of all my wisdom and inspiration. I am humbled by his faithfulness and the opportunity to share his Word with others.

To my tribe of family, beginning with my wife, Christy. Your unwavering support, encouragement, and prayers have been the driving force behind this project. You have been my constant companion, listening ear, and pillar of strength throughout the journey. Your love and belief in me have been a blessing beyond counting. To our three daughters, each of you contributed to this project in your own way. Alli, your unwavering discipline to the daily devotional practices motivates me in my own practice. Megan, your gift at crafting words into elegant and convicting messages inspires me to pursue my own writing. Casey, your fierce pursuit of justice and untiring practice of mercy stirs my conviction that living our beliefs is equally important as writing them. To my mom, Jan, not only did you provide valuable editing, your continual prayers and support were deeply felt.

A special thank you goes to my publisher, Sean Guillemette, for believing in this project and giving it the platform it needed to reach a wider audience. Your professionalism, expertise, and commitment to excellence have been instrumental in bringing this book to life. I am grateful for the opportunity to collaborate with you.

Lastly, I extend my heartfelt thanks to every reader who has chosen to embark on this devotional journey with me. Your openness, curiosity, and desire to deepen your faith are a testament to the power of God's Word. May his truth continue to resonate in your hearts and transform your lives. May the words within these pages bring hope, encouragement, and spiritual nourishment to all who read them.

Keep the Faith ~ A.B. DeBruyn

Welcome to a daily devotional that focuses exclusively on reading through the book of Romans. This letter by the Apostle Paul is his longest and most systematic writing about faith in Jesus. It is as deep as it is long and far more like a treatise than a letter. The words contained within have shaped and sharpened Christian theology, arguably more than any of his other works. This is important to our own theology. Theology is crucial to our faith because it guides and directs our thoughts, our words, and our actions. It connects what we believe to how we live.

Why "The Redeeming Road"?

I recently had the opportunity to travel to Spain to walk a portion of a 1,000-year-old pilgrimage known as the *Camino de Santiago* (translated: Way of St. James). I was provided the privilege of walking on actual Roman roads and crossing over Roman-built bridges. I couldn't help but be awestruck by their longevity, which is a testament to the enduring materials used and wondrous construction methods employed. At the same time, I was also surprised how they are still used on an everyday basis by people without much fuss or fanfare. To the locals, they are simply another resource in their life.

The book of Romans has that same solid and enduring construction. It too provides us with an invaluable resource in our life, but only if we are willing to utilize it. We should not be deterred by the size and complexity of this epistle. It is not a mountain to be scaled, but rather, a road to be walked. And like the *Camino,* it can only be done one day at a time, remembering that God *wants* to be known. He invites us into the task of discipleship as a way of expanding and enhancing our relationship with him. This is because Jesus never leaves us where he finds us. He is always beckoning us to explore life with him in new and stimulating ways.

How to Use This Devotional

The format for this devotional follows a structure that utilizes a repeating discipline of discipleship. Monday through Friday consists of a scripture reading, followed by a reflection, a few contemplation questions, and concludes with a short prayer. Saturday is focused exclusively on a longer prayer that revisits the themes of the week. Sunday is reserved for the sabbath and rest. Please note that the numbering for each entry accounts for Sundays, even though no entry is included.

To help in this, we will primarily be using two different bible translations. Eugene Peterson's paraphrase known as *The Message* (MSG) and the *Easy-to-Read Version* (ERV). I will lean heavily into the former because of the role it played in my own faith journey. I first encountered Peterson's work shortly after Jesus entered my life in 1997. It helped me immensely because he had a way of crafting the words in such a way as to soften the hard edges of the technical and scholastic tone of other translations while simultaneously not shying away from difficult theological issues. I also had the good fortune to spend a week in his presence and teaching in my first year of seminary. I firmly believe these two translations will serve as solid guideposts for our journey. Finally, there is a sprinkling of the *New International Version* (NIV) because oftentimes its use of wording will ring familiar to our ears. For the sake of clarity, a reference to which version is being used is provided in parentheses.

The devotional for each day will cite a portion of scripture for the day, but frequently, only an excerpt pertinent to the reflection is provided. This is for copyright reasons. However, let that serve as an invitation to read the noted scripture in its entirety in your own favored translation or even a variety of them. I am confident that the Holy Spirit will honor your efforts by illuminating other truths and realizations different from or beyond what I offer in my reflection section.

Encouragement

If you are a dedicated traveler, our journey through Romans will take 19 weeks over the course of 114 different entries. If you are more intermittent, it will take longer. However, like walking the *Camino de Santiago*, the key is not to get defeated in the journey. If you find that you have set this devotional down for whatever reason, then let me encourage you to always pick it back up and continue the trek. My hope is that God will be revealed as you are on *The Redeeming Road*.

Week 1

I, Paul, am a devoted slave of Jesus Christ on assignment...
(MSG)

1 Monday

Romans 1:1-7 (MSG)

I, Paul, am a devoted slave of Jesus Christ on assignment, authorized as an apostle to proclaim God's words and acts. I write this letter to all the believers in Rome, God's friends.

Reflection

Paul makes a simple, yet profound, statement in his opening sentence by calling himself a *slave* and an *apostle*. (Sidebar: Using these words is not artistic license by Peterson. They are original to Paul.) *Slave* is defined as being completely bound in the service of another, while *apostle* means having the role of a messenger or ambassador.

We read *slave* and *apostle* as two descriptors being in opposition to each other. We wonder how they can be spoken in the same breath, let alone about the same person. We recoil from the first and humbly defer from the second. But when Paul uses these two words, all he is doing is communicating his status and his purpose: a willing slave to Jesus and being set apart to share the Gospel, which, literally, is the *Good News* of God's saving grace.

How does this apply to us? Perhaps the trap is that we get stuck somewhere between these two descriptors. *Slave* is too lowly and degrading for our tastes. We abhor the thought of losing our freedom and being bonded in service to another. After all, we are immersed in a culture that idolizes personal liberty above all else. On the other hand, *apostle* is too lofty of a title. It suggests an aura of superiority, and secretly, we feel inadequate and unworthy. As a result, we become paralyzed in a "no man's land" filled with ambiguity and uncertainty. To overcome it, we need to grasp that Paul is not unique in his status and purpose. On the contrary, it is what all of us who identify as Christ-followers hold in common: we have a kinship with Jesus, and we are given purpose as ambassadors for the kingdom.

Contemplation Questions

1. What invitations has God extended to you for a role in his kingdom?

_____

_____

_____

_____

2. How would you describe that role? Slave, or servant, or something else?

_____

_____

_____

_____

3. What influence does your answer to the previous question have on your self-worth?

_____

_____

_____

_____

Lord Jesus, we embrace our being bonded to you as *slaves* and yet, crowned by you as *apostles*. Humble us in your grace. Strengthen us in your love. Encourage us through the Holy Spirit as we step into this new day.

Amen.

2 Tuesday

Romans 1:8-12 (ERV)

First I want to say that I thank my God through Jesus Christ for all of you. I thank him because people everywhere in the world are talking about your great faith. Every time I pray, I always remember you. God knows this is true.

Reflection

There are positive vibes emanating from Paul's words. There is an upbeat tone to it. It is a warm invitation full of reassurance and love, so we naturally gravitate toward it. This is not surprising since our culture places a strong emphasis on experiencing "happiness." In fact, we can trace back to the founding of our country since the Declaration of Independence asserts the "pursuit of happiness" is one of our inalienable rights.

Nothing is wrong with being happy, but that emotion has an extremely short shelf life. It just doesn't last very long. As a result, similar to an addiction, we can quickly find ourselves searching for the next "fix" of happiness that might manifest itself in all sorts of unhealthy ways. So we should pursue it with a bit of skepticism.

Paul's opening greeting to his readers isn't really about pursuing happiness. Rather, it is about *fulfillment*, and that is an important distinction. Fulfillment is found in his status and purpose; or in leadership lingo, he discovered the WHY behind the WHAT. God extends the same invitation to us: to discover the fullness of who he created us to be. If we accept that invitation, what we will learn is that the experience of fulfillment runs deeper and lasts longer than happiness. It combines both what we *feel* and what we *know* about ourselves. It occurs when we recognize, and rest into, the knowledge and security that we are not alone, but instead, are an integral part of an expanding intrusion of God's kingdom into our world. To accomplish it, to borrow from Eugene Peterson, we must "undermine the kingdom of self and establish the kingdom of God."

Contemplation Questions

1. What intrusions of the kingdom do you detect happening in your life? How are you responding to them?

_____

_____

_____

_____

2. If you examine your motivations, are you seeking happiness or fulfillment?

_____

_____

_____

_____

3. How might you "undermine the kingdom of self"?

_____

_____

_____

_____

> Holy Spirit, illuminate for us the "why" behind the things and feelings we are pursuing. Give us discernment so we may know if we are chasing personal happiness or seeking fulfillment in you. Humble us in your grace. Strengthen us in your love. Encourage us as we step into this new day.
>
> Amen.

3   Wednesday

Romans 1:13-17 (MSG)

Please don't misinterpret my failure to visit you, friends. You have no idea how many times I've made plans for Rome. I've been determined to get some personal enjoyment out of God's work among you, as I have in so many other non-Jewish towns and communities. But something has always come up and prevented it.

Reflection

For most of us, life is consumed with preparing for our future. The extent of that planning can be long-range goals of career and family, to the immediacy of pulling together a shopping list for a meal tonight. Yet, we quickly learn that even our best-laid plans are frequently interrupted, redirected, or canceled. As our scripture for today reveals, this is true for Paul as it is for us. His best intentions to visit people he dearly loves are thwarted.

These kinds of interruptions and redirections happen all too frequently for us as well. At a minimum, it is a frustrating experience. At its worst, it feels defeating and hopeless–even to the extent of blaming God and maybe even seeing him as our enemy…at least to our hopes and aspirations. In those moments, where do we turn? Do we adapt or do we quit? Do we adjust or do we become stubborn? There is no pat answer because each circumstance is unique. However, one strategy that always works for me is to ask a simple question: "What is the invitation here, Lord?"

This strategy is demonstrated in our scripture passage, albeit subtly. In Paul's words of excuse and explanation, God is communicating the same invitation to us. We can see it when we think about what might have happened–or not happened–had Paul relentlessly and obstinately pursued his original plan to go to Rome. The very scripture we are reading some 2,000 years later would never have been written.

We should always entertain the possibility that God is seeking to accomplish something greater with our circumstances than what we realize, especially in those moments when it appears that nothing is going according to *our* plan. God is always beckoning us toward him. We are always welcomed into his presence, but more so, into his perfect will. This means that even if our carefully prepared plan has been constructed in faithful obedience, sometimes God sends us in a different direction, turns us around, or stops us altogether. In those moments, we need to ask God about his invitation. We will never see God's invitation until we have eyes to look for it.

Contemplation Questions

1. Where have your intentions and plans been stopped or diverted?

2. Have you ever considered asking God about his invitation at that moment?

3. Is that moment happening even now as you read this?

> Heavenly Father, forgive us our attitudes of stubbornness or feelings of defeat when life does not unfold to our preconceived plans. Remind us that you always welcome us into your presence and enfold us into your perfect will. Humble us in your grace. Strengthen us in your love. Encourage us as we step into this new day.
>
> Amen.

4   Thursday

Romans 1:18-25 (ERV)

God shows his anger from heaven against all the evil and wrong things that people do. Their evil lives hide the truth they have. This makes God angry because they have been shown what he is like. Yes, God has made it clear to them.

Reflection

Anger, like love, is one of the more intense human emotions. When we are angry, our heart rate and blood pressure go up, as do the levels of hormones, adrenaline, and all the other mysterious chemicals flowing through our bloodstream. It is a full-body experience. Also, like love, anger is only experienced in response to situations we care about and are important to us. Finally, anger never *feels* wrong in the moment. When it happens, we process it as *righteous* anger.

However, the big distinction between the two is that, unlike love, human anger, in its heightened state, frequently causes us to become aggressive…and that usually means someone else is on the receiving end of that aggression. Most of us know what it feels like to be the target of anger, and it is never pleasant. In fact, many times it feels scary and unsafe. As a result, our typical reaction is to separate or insulate ourselves from that person and their anger.

But what do we feel when we read about God's anger? My observation is that many of us equate God's anger as being the same as human anger, except on a larger scale. It is more intense. It is more aggressive. And worst of all, we assume someone is going to be on the receiving end of it…and it might very well be us. That thought can trigger us to react instinctively by employing the same strategies of trying to feel safe by creating physical and emotional distance. That would be a mistake.

God's anger is not like flawed human anger. While it is truly righteous, it is not aggressive. On the contrary, it is restrained and patient. While God still hates sin and the destruction that sin inevitably leaves in its wake, we can trust that he will not act violently against us. This is because the ultimate impact of sin, death, has already been dealt with through the work of Jesus on the cross. His act of sacrifice gives us not only the strength but the privilege to stand in the presence of God *and* his anger. We do not have to separate or insulate *from* it, but rather, learn and repent *because* of it.

Contemplation Questions

1. How do you imagine God's anger? Do you equate it with the traits and expressions of human anger? Why or why not?

___

2. What reactions do you imagine you have to God's anger? Would it turn you toward him or away from him?

___

3. Do you detect God's love and purpose underlying his expression of anger?

___

> Heavenly Father, we know that your anger is directed toward our sin and its consequences. But we also know that your love is even bigger. Through your limitless forgiveness, you will set all things right. Humble us in your grace. Strengthen us in your love. Encourage us as we step into this new day.
>
> Amen.

5   Friday

Romans 1:26-32 (MSG)

Since they didn't bother to acknowledge God, God quit bothering them and let them run loose. And then all hell broke loose: rampant evil, grabbing and grasping, vicious backstabbing. They made life hell on earth with their envy, wanton killing, bickering, and cheating. Look at them: mean-spirited, venomous, fork-tongued God-bashers. Bullies, swaggerers, insufferable windbags! They keep inventing new ways of wrecking lives.

Reflection

There are days that I refuse to look at the news feed coming to me via the internet because the events that are reported are so disheartening. A never-ending stream of negative reports on the status and direction of the world gives rise to despair and hopelessness. The strategy of closing my eyes to that reality only provides temporary respite. When I open my eyes again, little or nothing has changed.

It would be easy to blame the advent of digital communication and connection for this problem. But that is nothing more than, metaphorically speaking, blaming the messenger. The events Paul describes in our scripture passage have always been present in our world since Adam and Eve exited the garden. Our world has been, is, and will always be broken until Christ returns.

What do we do in the middle of this ever-increasing chaos and devastation? How do we survive, let alone respond? The direction scripture gives us is not in the form of a directive but rather by way of contrast. Paul points out the natural consequence of refusing to know God and the result that flows from it–turning away from him. The litany of sins Paul spells out are the natural effect of Adam and Eve's original sin: wanting to know the difference between good and evil. In so doing, humanity decided to no longer learn from God, but instead, make its own decisions on what is right and wrong. Humanity fools itself into thinking this will make us more like God, when in fact, it makes us more like Satan. The proof of that truth is found in today's (and each day's) news feed.

The better response then is to keep our eyes open. While we need to recognize the reality of our news feed, we shouldn't become enamored with it. Instead, we must give priority to turning our eyes toward God, in which our hope and joy rest. It is God who is the author of truth and who will ultimately redeem the world. As the psalmist tells us in Psalm 16, "I keep my eyes on the Lord. With him at my side, I will not be shaken." The invitation is to always be ready and willing to return toward the one who forgives, saves, and redeems.

Contemplation Questions

1. How much attention each day do you devote to current events?

2. Are you paying attention to how this is impacting you?

3. What influence does the news cycle have on your discipleship practices?

> Lord Jesus, we are surrounded by a broken world. Our thoughts struggle to grasp the extent of violence and hurt we inflict on each other. Our hearts grieve for the injustice and suffering these acts cause. We just want to close our eyes. Jesus, gently open our eyes so we can see the reality, not just the brokenness, but also your coming redemption. Humble us in your grace. Strengthen us in your love. Encourage us as we step into this new day.
>
> Amen.

6   Saturday

Father, Son, and Holy Spirit:

We are bonded to you as *slaves*, and yet, crowned by you as *apostles*.

We ask for illumination and understanding, self-awareness, and proper perspective.

Wash away our pride and stubbornness and redeem our losses and defeats. Remind us of your sovereignty and supremacy and that your plan is better than our plan.

Give us hope and purpose in the midst of our broken world. Tell us again that we are always welcomed into your presence and that you will enfold us into your perfect will.

Through your unlimited forgiveness, you will set all things right. Our fulfillment is only found in you.

Humble us in your grace. Strengthen us in your love. Encourage us as we step into this new day.

Amen.

Week 1

Pyrenees Mountains, Spain

Week 2

Every time you criticize someone, you condemn yourself.
(MSG)

8 — Monday

Romans 2:1-4 (MSG)

Every time you criticize someone, you condemn yourself. It takes one to know one. Judgmental criticism of others is a well-known way of escaping detection in your own crimes and misdemeanors. But God isn't so easily diverted. He sees right through all such smoke screens and holds you to what *you've* done…God is kind, but he's not soft. In kindness he takes us firmly by the hand and leads us into a radical life-change.

Reflection

It is the human condition to navigate our lives with the subconscious understanding that we live at the center of our own universe. What we think of as "the world" is actually quite limited. Most of what we understand and process can only be done from our own exclusive perspective. Events and experiences are like stage props; they constantly move into our sightline, but then fade over the time horizon as we pass through. This has a subtle, but important, impact on our viewpoint. It can manifest itself in two primary, but opposite, ways.

On one end of the spectrum is using the tactic of "deflection." We do this when we readily acknowledge that the world surrounding us is broken but are less willing to recognize that we are inherently part of that brokenness. We ignore our own sins by pointing at those of others. We dwell on what is amiss with the world and others instead of examining our own faults. We cast ourselves as part of the solution and not the problem.

On the opposite end of the spectrum is the way of "absorption." We become obsessed with our own faults and shortcomings to the point of becoming paralyzed. We recognize the brokenness of the world, but it pales against our own flaws. We still engage in comparing, but it only results in our own despairing. We are the problem and there is no solution.

Both perspectives are unhealthy, and they illustrate significant deficits of self-awareness and emotional intelligence. They are also unbiblical. Scripture unhesitatingly tells us that we *are* part of the problem, but we can also participate in the solution so long as we have the right perspective. Our scripture passage captures this truth: "God is kind, but he's not soft. In kindness he takes us firmly by the hand and leads us into a radical life-change."

If we let ourselves be fully infused with the grace and love of Jesus, we can realistically see our sins and stop "deflecting." It also allows us to be transformed into the fullness of who God created us to be so we can stop "absorbing." This will allow us to shift our view of the center of the universe to its proper place: God the Father. We will be relieved to know that the universe rests safely in his strong hands.

Contemplation Questions

1. How would you describe your personal self-awareness?

_____

_____

_____

_____

2. Are you conscious of your limited horizon for seeing "the world"? Can you detect the limitations of experiencing it only from our own perspective?

_____

_____

_____

_____

3. Do you notice when you "deflect" or "absorb" your brokenness? What adjustments can you make to have a healthier self-perception?

_____

_____

_____

_____

> Heavenly Father, forgive us for our continued self-focused ways of moving through the life you have gifted us with. Remind us of your sovereignty and supremacy. Humble us in your grace. Strengthen us in your love. Encourage us as we step into this new day.
>
> Amen.

9   Tuesday

Romans 2:5-11 (MSG)

God pays no attention to what others say (or what you think) about you. He makes up his own mind.

Reflection

There is a poignant line in the movie *The Big Short* which tells the story of the financial collapse of the American housing market in 2008. "Truth is like poetry. And most people [absolutely] hate poetry." There are all kinds of truths floating around in the world, but perhaps the biggest one we reject and avoid is about ourselves. Unpoetically, we painstakingly build a self-image that has some truth to it, but also contains a fair amount of falsehoods and ignorance. We want to "look the part" or "dress for success." We do this because we are always living in our own presence, and sometimes we can't stand the company. It is understandable. To continuously carry the full brunt of the truth about ourselves is almost unbearable.

    The mirror, they say, never lies. If we want to discover who we really are inside, we need to look into an accurate mirror. The Bible is that mirror. Scripture has a way of reflecting a correct and complete picture of who we are, and who we are not. It can (and should) cause our false self-image to collapse, which is painful, but necessary.

    Yet not everything that stares back at us is deflating or defeating. God cares about who we are and not a whit for what we think our appearance should be. God examines our heart, because as Proverbs 4:23 points out, everything flows from it. He reminds us that we are his beloved child, carefully and lovingly crafted. The life he gives us has opportunities for purpose, community, and sufficiency. If we accept and adopt what God tells us about ourselves, we can start living a "real life."

Contemplation Questions

1. Do you believe you have an accurate picture of yourself? Are you open to the observations of others about yourself?

   _____

   _____

   _____

   _____

2. When you describe yourself to someone, what do you include or leave out?

   _____

   _____

   _____

   _____

3. How would God's description of you be different from your own self-description?

   _____

   _____

   _____

   _____

> Heavenly Father, remind us of who we are and who we are not. Hold the mirror before us so we can see how dependent we are on you. Reclaim us in your grace. Rebuild us in your love. Reform us into your perfect plan as we step into this new day.
>
> Amen.

10 — Wednesday

Romans 2:12-16 (MSG)

If you sin without knowing what you're doing, God takes that into account. But if you sin knowing full well what you're doing, that's a different story entirely. Merely hearing God's law is a waste of your time if you don't do what he commands. Doing, not hearing, is what makes the difference with God.

Reflection

There is an ongoing and endless debate in sociology and psychology on whether humanity has innate morality. Are we born with a sense of right and wrong, or are we taught it? Theologians then jump into the debate with the question of whether those who never have the opportunity to hear about Jesus can still receive salvation? Does right living merit an invitation into the kingdom as being "good enough?"

All of these questions are worthy of exploration, which is to be expected. Humanity has always been intensely curious. Not only do we want to discover *how* things work, but *why*. That curiosity is both a strength and a weakness. It has led to vast improvements in the quality of life, but it also led to us being removed from the Garden of Eden. As such, we must be mindful to what degree we pursue our questions and the answers we deduce.

When we bring that same intensity of curiosity to the gift of God's salvation, there is a strength and weakness in exploring the "how" and "why" of saving grace. On the one hand, we can reassure those who may doubt or are in crisis. We are reminded that the promises of God are immutable and unbreakable. He can be trusted. On the other hand, we run the risk of fooling ourselves into thinking that the "system of salvation" can, at best, be reduced to a safe recipe of reciting the right words. At worst, we are capable of being manipulated in favor of our allies or leveraged against our perceived enemies.

Our scripture reminds us that while God wants to be known to us, we will never know everything about him. And while God seeks to be in relationship with us, he does not do so at the expense of his sovereignty. The gift of salvation from the ruler of the universe will not be diminished to mere procedure. It ignores the reality about God that the psalmist tells us plainly: "He is in the heavens and he does whatever pleases him" (Psalm 115). Or in the words of Mr. Beaver in C.S. Lewis's classic *The Lion, the Witch, and the Wardrobe*, "Who said anything about safe? 'Course he isn't safe. But he's good. He's the King, I tell you.'"

Week 2

Contemplation Questions

1. How comfortable are you with not knowing everything about God?

___

___

___

___

2. If you could ask God one question and get an answer, what would it be?

___

___

___

___

3. What impact on your faith would his answer bring you?

___

___

___

___

> Heavenly Father, you, indeed, are in the heavens, but that does not mean your presence is removed from us. We praise you for your glorious gift of salvation, and we seek forgiveness for every instance when we don't treat that gift with the reverence it rightfully deserves. Reclaim us in your grace. Rebuild us in your love. Reform us into your perfect plan as we step into this new day.
>
> Amen.

11   Thursday

Romans 2:17-24 (MSG)

If you're brought up Jewish, don't assume that you can lean back in the arms of your religion and take it easy, feeling smug because you're an insider to God's revelation, a connoisseur of the best things of God, informed on the latest doctrines! I have a special word of caution for you who are sure that you have it all together yourselves and, because you know God's revealed Word inside and out, feel qualified to guide others through their blind alleys and dark nights and confused emotions to God. While you are guiding others, who is going to guide you?

Reflection

In the original context of the book of Romans, the concept of Christianity was in its infancy, if not nonexistent. Yet, it still speaks to us in the here and now. It reveals a timeless truth about humanity's penchant for organizing ourselves into tribes of insiders and treating everyone else as outsiders. We do this in everything from ethnicity to politics to our favorite sports teams…and perhaps nowhere more than in our view of faith. In our reading for today, we only need to substitute the word "Jewish" with "Christian," and immediately we find ourselves being convicted by what is being expressed.

    As Christians, we place an emphasis on the power and comfort of faith. It shields us, especially in times of stress, pain, or uncertainty. But when we become overly comfortable in our faith, thinking we have an exclusive insider view of how things are, we wield it as a sword. It becomes a potential weapon for inflicting harm, not only toward others but ourselves as well. We brandish it with false confidence, ignoring or covering our own sin and shame in the process. We treat faith not as a gift but as an entitlement. At that moment, "outsiders frown on God" because of our attitude.

    Every day we should strive to wake up in humility and repentance. Faith not only requires us to ask for forgiveness, but to extend it to others. Faith not only requires us to rely on God's provision, but to share it generously. Faith not only requires us to seek God's plan, but to obediently follow it once it is revealed. Faith is a reward not a right. When we seek the Lord with all our heart, mind, soul, and strength, everything else that is necessary will be added.

Contemplation Questions

1. As a Christian, what situations or contexts make you an "outsider"?

_____

_____

_____

_____

2. What do you notice about the ways you think and react in those situations?

_____

_____

_____

_____

3. Are you aware of God's presence in that context? If so, how? Answer the same questions replacing the word "outsider" with "insider."

_____

_____

_____

_____

> Holy Father, forgive our complacency and lazy practice of faith. Pardon our sins and refresh our attitude to see you rightly as sovereign over our lives. Reclaim us in your grace. Rebuild us in your love. Reform us into your perfect plan as we step into this new day.
>
> Amen.

12 Friday

Romans 2:25-29 (ERV)

You are not a true Jew if you are only a Jew in your physical body. True circumcision is not only on the outside of the body. A true Jew is one who is a Jew inside. True circumcision is done in the heart. It is done by the Spirit, not by the written law. And anyone who is circumcised in the heart by the Spirit gets praise from God, not from people.

Reflection

The Jewish ordinance of circumcision is a sign and seal of the covenant God made with Abraham. As a mark of ritual purity, it set them apart from the surrounding cultures. Most Jewish men interpret circumcision as a privilege and not mutilation. But as with all sacred symbols, they are of little benefit if the underlying value it seeks to communicate is not adopted and internalized.

As Christians, baptism is the sign and seal of our justification through Jesus. But like circumcision, it is a privilege not an ordinance. If the cleansing of our sin doesn't lead us toward transformation, it is nothing more than a dousing of water. Jesus himself highlighted the importance of not letting the symbol supersede the intent when he said that the sabbath was created for humanity, not the other way around.

To be "holy" is literally defined as "to be set apart." It means to be reserved as something unique and special. From God's perspective, the Holy Spirit being active in our hearts, guiding our thoughts, words, actions, and reactions is the essence of what "sets us apart" from the surrounding world. The symbol's only purpose is to reinforce that reality. But it is a privilege not an ordinance. Our task is to be aware of the privilege and step into it as a reality.

Week 2

Contemplation Questions

1. How do you receive encouragement in your faith? Is baptism one of the ways?

___

2. If baptism sets us apart, how often do you find yourself relying on that reality? Why?

___

3. In what ways has God made you unique and special? How do you connect your unique and special attributes to being made holy?

___

> Jesus, through your love and sacrifice, you have marked us as Holy and set us apart from wickedness. You have invited us into the new reality of your kingdom. Reclaim us in your grace. Rebuild us in your love. Reform us into your perfect plan as we step into this new day.
>
> Amen.

13   Saturday

Father God, Jesus Son, and Holy Spirit:

Remind us of our identity. Give us eyes to see who we are and who we are not. Hold the mirror before us so we can see how dependent we are on you.

Lord, remind us that although you are in the heavens, you are always present with us. Your gift of salvation will not be taken from us but forgive us when we don't treat it with the reverence it rightfully deserves.

Be patient with our complacency and laziness. Pardon our sins and refresh our attitude to see you rightly as sovereign over our lives.

Jesus, we recall that through your love and sacrifice, you have marked us as holy and set us apart from wickedness. You have invited us into the dance of faith, and we move to the beat of your kingdom. Give us the wisdom and fortitude to remain in step with you.

Reclaim us in your grace. Rebuild us in your love. Reform us into your perfect plan as we step into this new day.

Amen.

Week 2

Saint-Michel, France

Week 3

Do you think their faithlessness cancels out his faithfulness?
(MSG)

15   Monday

Romans 3:1-8 (MSG)

Do you think their faithlessness cancels out his faithfulness? Not on your life! Depend on it: God keeps his word even when the whole world is lying through its teeth. Scripture says the same:

> Your words stand fast and true;
> Rejection doesn't faze you.

Reflection

Theology—literally the study of God—faces the impossible task of trying to wrap our arms around the infinite. We can't possibly do it, but that doesn't mean we shouldn't try. We strive to better understand the ways and means of our Father while acknowledging he already knows us better than we know ourselves. From our side of it, getting to know God better is the very nature of relationship building. From God's side of it, slowly and patiently waiting for us to know him is the very nature of love. It is a prolonged dance of discovery, and it requires both intimacy and endurance.

If we call this dance by its proper name—faith—a critical step in its movement is known as *obedience*. It is the redirecting of our inherently selfish desires towards God's unselfish will. So often we view obedience as a drudging subservience or the antithesis of freedom. But submission to God's leading is not simply giving into stifling patriarchy. Rather, it is an intentional and humble act of deference.

Dancing to our own music is not freedom but chaos. Dancing in step with God reveals his beauty and majesty, and at the same time, the fullness of who he created us to be: his dance partner.

Contemplation Questions

1. Describe the ways you "try to wrap your arms around God"?

   _____
   _____
   _____
   _____

2. Where do you detect and perceive God wrapping his arms around you?

   _____
   _____
   _____
   _____

3. What can you do today to better stay in step with God's leading?

   _____
   _____
   _____
   _____

Heavenly Father, you lead and guide us in the dance of faith. Give us the wisdom and fortitude to remain in step with you. Reclaim us in your grace. Rebuild us in your love. Reform us into your perfect plan as we step into this new day.

Amen.

16   Tuesday

Romans 3:9-20 (MSG)

So where does that put us? Do we Jews get a better break than the others? Not really. Basically, all of us, whether insiders or outsiders, start out in identical conditions, which is to say that we all start out as sinners. Scripture leaves no doubt about it:

> There's nobody living right, not even one,
>   nobody who knows the score, nobody
>   alert for God.

Reflection

In the human race, none of us begin at the same starting line. Some are born with vitality while others struggle just to draw breath. Some are welcomed into safe and nurturing homes, others into chaos and dysfunction. Some have the benefit of safe communities and opportunities for advancement, others are refugees facing displacement and poverty.

But there is one starting line in life that we all share: being born into sin. The truth about sin is that it ignores all barriers of geography, ethnicity, or context. It does not discern or discriminate based on our family of origin, social status, or education. Sin is the great equalizer of us all.

Just as much as God hates our sins, he loves *all* of us. We are reminded that none of us stands higher than the other in front of God. So, while it is true that we are set free from the consequences of sin through the sacrifice of Jesus, that does not elevate our position above our fellow humans. When we recognize the reality that we do indeed share this most significant starting point, it allows us to see others in the same light as we see ourselves, to value them as we value ourselves, and ultimately to love them as we love ourselves. It is then we discover the starting point of the Great Commandment.

Contemplation Questions

1. How would you describe your "starting line" in life?

   _____

   _____

   _____

   _____

2. What do you notice about your reaction toward other people with different social status, education, or place of origin?

   _____

   _____

   _____

   _____

3. Do you find that you are more focused on your sins or the sins of others? How does that influence your love for yourself and toward others?

   _____

   _____

   _____

   _____

> Heavenly Father, none of us stand above another. We are all laid low by our sins. Instill in us a sense of humility toward one another so that we may demonstrate your affection for all of us. Recover us through your grace. Restore us in your love. Reveal your presence among us as we step into this new day.
>
> Amen.

17   Wednesday

Romans 3:21-24 (ERV)

But God has a way to make people right, and it has nothing to do with the law. He has now shown us that new way, which the law and the prophets told us about. God makes people right through their faith in Jesus Christ. He does this for all who believe in Christ. Everyone is the same. All have sinned and are not good enough to share God's divine greatness. They are made right with God by his grace. This is a free gift. They are made right with God by being made free from sin through Jesus Christ.

Reflection

If we all share the same "starting line" of sin, we also all share the same "finish line" of life in Jesus. While that shared equality with our fellow human beings might be of some comfort, we must not reduce the practice of faith to a race between start and finish.

A race conjures visions of competition and prizes, of victors and also-rans. While faith, like a race, involves striving and yearning, it is not a contest. It is more than exerting ourselves for accomplishment; it is having the humility to recognize our own incapacity. Faith is not an outward battle to win an award; it is an inward tranquility of accepting a gift.

When we undertake the practices of faith, it reveals a deeper understanding that the race has already been won. It is not up to us to race *toward* Jesus, but rather, to intentionally slow down and travel *with* Jesus.

Contemplation Questions

1. On a scale of 1 to 10 (10 being highest), how would you rate your competitiveness?

   _____
   _____
   _____
   _____

2. How does your level of competitiveness influence your practice of faith?

   _____
   _____
   _____

3. Describe one step that you can take to enhance calmness in your faith practice. How can you be held accountable for taking that step?

   _____
   _____
   _____
   _____

> Lord Jesus, forgive us for when we reduce our faith to a competitive race, both against others and against ourselves. While we strive in our discipleship, remind us that the invitation is always to live a life with you. Recover us through your grace. Restore us in your love. Reveal your presence among us as we step into this new day.
>
> Amen.

18 — Thursday

Romans 3:25-26 (MSG)

God sacrificed Jesus on the altar of the world to clear that world of sin. Having faith in him sets us in the clear. God decided on this course of action in full view of the public—to set the world in the clear with himself through the sacrifice of Jesus, finally taking care of the sins he had so patiently endured.

Reflection

When humanity was removed from God's presence, it was never his plan to make that banishment permanent. The desire of God was, is, and will always be, restoring the intimate relationship he once enjoyed with us. The Old Testament spells out his amazingly patient efforts in trying to bring us, his children, back to himself. Indeed, that the scripture even refers to us as "his children" should make that desire abundantly clear.

Unwearyingly, he presented opportunity after opportunity for the covenant people to repent and return to him. The invitation was constantly extended with countless chances for his people to accept. He was giving his children an opening to make the first move, if only so it felt like it was their decision. Yet, history makes it equally clear that they always resisted.

Then the nature of the invitation changed. It was made infinitely more simple and incredibly more personal. The invitation came through God's one and only son, Jesus. From that moment, and all the moments that have since followed, the relationship is restored only through the son. But the invitation remains the same. We call that invitation faith. If we accept and practice faith, the banishment is revoked, and the relationship is restored.

Contemplation Questions

1. Where do you detect your own reluctance or indifference toward intimacy with God?

2. If God invites us into an intimate relationship, describe what that intimacy looks like for you.

3. What spiritual practices are you familiar with or have experience that can nurture your intimate relationship with God?

> Heavenly Father, forgive our stubbornness. We continue in the ways of Adam and Eve by deciding for ourselves what is good and evil. Dissolve our hubris. Remind us of your invitation for a relationship through faith. Recover us through your grace. Restore us in your love. Reveal your presence among us as we step into this new day.
>
> Amen.

19   Friday

Romans 3:27-31 (MSG)

What we've learned is this: God does not respond to what *we* do; we respond to what *God* does. We've finally figured it out. Our lives get in step with God and all others by letting him set the pace, not by proudly or anxiously trying to run the parade.

Reflection

A popular bumper sticker/meme reads: "God is my co-pilot." It reflects the mindset that God is beside us, but we are the ones flying the airplane. This perspective is helpful in that it highlights our involvement and responsibility for how we navigate daily living. Indeed, it would be far worse to suggest that God is the pilot, and we are merely passengers stuck in the economy section at the back of the plane. We have a critical role in setting the direction and pace of our lives. The challenge is where we fit God into that perspective.

If we continue the metaphor, we need to remember that God is the one who constructed the airplane in the first place. He is the one who fueled it and created the air that it flies through. In other words, God graces us with life, and he gives us the privileges of stewardship over it. While he is beside us as we make choices, decisions, and reactions in our piloting, it is not the *only* place God is present. He is omnipresent and universal, which is to say, God is *everywhere*. This is his creation, and he firmly remains in control of it all.

As our scripture for today urges, when we have the elements of our faith life in its "proper place," our course is more easily charted. We let God set the course, and then we follow it.

Contemplation Questions

1. How would you describe your current sense of control over your life? Where do you detect God's presence and power in the midst of your current situation?

   _____
   _____
   _____
   _____

2. What is your sense of God's invitation over the issue of control? Is it to exert more or surrender to less control?

   _____
   _____
   _____
   _____

3. If you were to take affirmative steps to surrender control to God, what would they be? Identify and examine your expectations from taking those steps.

   _____
   _____
   _____
   _____

> Heavenly Father, we have the honor of being at your right hand. We are adrift and we look to you to correct our course. Recover us through your grace. Restore us in your love. Reveal your presence among us as we step into this new day.
>
> Amen.

20 — Saturday

The Redeeming Road

Heavenly Father, Lord Jesus, and Holy Spirit:

Remind us that none of us stand above another. We are all laid low by our sins. Forgive us for all the times when we turned the practice of faith into a competitive race, both against others and against ourselves. Out of sheer stubbornness, we continue in the ways of Adam and Eve by deciding for ourselves what is good and evil or when we expect compensation for our obedience.

Be patient with us as we strive in our discipleship. Let us see it properly for what it is: an invitation to live life with you. As we pursue our faith, dissolve our pride. Instill in us a sense of humility toward our fellow people so that we may demonstrate your affection for all of us. Prompt us in the honor we enjoy of being at your right hand.

Finally, Lord, let us recall that your gift of grace was achieved at a cost none of us could ever pay. May all that we say and do be motivated only by our thankfulness and nothing else.

Recover us through your grace. Restore us in your love. Reveal your presence among us as we step into this new day.

Amen.

Castildelgado, Spain

Week 4

When people work, their pay is not given to them as a gift.
(ERV)

22 Monday

Romans 4:1-5 (ERV)

When people work, their pay is not given to them as a gift. They earn the pay they get. But people cannot do any work that will make them right with God. So they must trust in him. Then he accepts their faith, and that makes them right with him. He is the one who makes even evil people right.

Reflection

In the economy of the kingdom, good produces more good, just as evil produces more evil. So pursuing good and doing right is always the desired choice, and blessings will flow from that decision. But sometimes, maybe many times, our subjective experience is that we're not seeing any benefit from our hard work and sacrifice. So why even try?

When blessings flow from right actions, we have to recognize that many times we will not detect or discern that blessing. Yes, we could say that it is like a direct deposit into our "blessing bank account," but it is solely up to God on how the wages get "paid." We need to recognize that God puts the fruit of our good work toward places where it is most needed, not where we might most desire it.

This is why the more valuable currency in the kingdom is trust. Trust doesn't require any "work" on our part. Either we trust, or we don't. When we trust with confidence that God is who he says he is, and acts like he promises he will act, then the vaults holding God's blessings will open wide, and it is credited to us as righteousness.

Contemplation Questions

1. What good in thought, word, or deed might God be inviting you into today?

   _____
   _____
   _____
   _____

2. Do you expect a blessing from God as a return for your obedience or sacrifice?

   _____
   _____
   _____
   _____

3. What does "trust in God" look or feel like in your faith for today?

   _____
   _____
   _____
   _____

> Father, we pursue good and rightness out of our gratitude for what you have already done for us. May your blessings flow as you direct them. But Lord, in the midst of the hard and the painful, may we place all our trust in you. Humble us in your grace. Strengthen us in your love. Encourage us as we step into this new day.
>
> Amen.

23 — Tuesday

Romans 4:6-9 (MSG)

David confirms this way of looking at it, saying that the one who trusts God to do the putting-everything-right without insisting on having a say in it is one fortunate man:

Fortunate those whose crimes are
> whisked away,
> whose sins are wiped clean from the
> > slate.

Fortunate the person against
> whom the Lord does not keep score.

Reflection

The scripture for today quotes the first two verses of Psalm 32. Those words were written by David following his confession to God of his awful sin of arranging for the death of Bathsheba's husband so he could take her as his wife. The words capture not only thanksgiving, but David's trust in God. He knew he didn't have a single fact to lean on in his defense, but he trusted in the Father's response of mercy when he owned his failures. God, true to his promises, forgave him.

We should not gloss over David's sin without hesitation. It was a horrible and despicable crime. To be dismissive of it as a plot device in a story we've become too familiar with is to miss the gravity of the transgression, and more importantly, the astounding response of grace. David certainly didn't make that mistake. He understood that confession was a key component to receiving forgiveness from God, but he also knew it required trust.

For us, we tend to treat our sins in two ways: 1) we either pay too little heed to some, believing God will simply clean up after us without the necessity of our confession, and 2) we hang on to others, convinced that we cannot rely on God to forgive us. Both are unhealthy and unbiblical practices as either prevent the fullness of righteousness. Confession welcomes the gift of our forgiveness, and trust is the catalyst that solidifies our faith.

Contemplation Questions

1. What sins are you reluctant to confess to, or seek forgiveness for?

_____
_____
_____
_____

2. Reflect on the reasons holding you back from offering them to God.

_____
_____
_____
_____

3. Have you repeatedly confessed a particular sin, but your belief or actions haven't changed? If so, what gets in the way of experiencing transformation?

_____
_____
_____
_____

> Lord Jesus, may we always return to you in full repentance. Let us trust you with all of our sins and shortcomings. Humble us in your grace. Strengthen us in your love. Encourage us as we step into this new day.
>
> Amen.

24 Wednesday

Romans 4:10-12 (MSG)

Now *think:* Was that declaration made before or after he was marked by the covenant rite of circumcision? That's right, *before* he was marked. That means that he underwent circumcision as evidence and confirmation of what God had done long before to bring him into this acceptable standing with himself, an act of God he had embraced with his whole life.

Reflection

We all have a father and mother, grandparents, great-grandparents…as far back as we can trace. Even if we are adopted, we all have a family history. Their DNA can be traced back to our own. Similarly, their decisions of who they loved, where they lived, and what they did had a direct impact on the trajectory of our own life. In large part, we are now because of who they were then.

This is also true of our faith. Some of us have families who own a strong pedigree in the faith–we were reared in the church. Others of us didn't have the benefit of that kind of nurturing–the concept of church was foreign and unappealing. Yet others of us had a bad experience with religion, finding it neither welcoming or inspiring, and we orphaned ourselves from it. Like our DNA, we all bring an indelible family and personal history into our faith. The question is how much credence we give it.

The truth that Paul expresses is that when it comes to God, our family lineage carries no influence. As the old saying goes "God has no grandchildren." We cannot trust and rely on the faith of our family as being sufficient or to serve as an excuse. In our relationship with God, there are no human go-betweens.

Contemplation Questions

1. How has your family history impacted your relationship with God? Has it been a benefit or a hindrance?

_____

_____

_____

_____

2. When and where was God in the midst of your family history?

_____

_____

_____

_____

3. How might God be inviting you into a deeper connection with him that builds upon, or rises above, your family history with the faith?

_____

_____

_____

_____

> Heavenly Father, you created all of us, and knit us together into a history of a family. May we be wise enough to embrace the strength and shed the weakness of it. Let it not be either our reliance or our alibi. Remind us that you are our Father, and there is no other like you. Humble us in your grace. Strengthen us in your love. Encourage us as we step into this new day.
>
> Amen.

25   Thursday

Romans 4:13-15 (MSG)

If those who get what God gives them only get it by doing everything they are told to do and filling out all the right forms properly signed, that eliminates personal trust completely and turns the promise into an ironclad *contract*! That's not a holy promise; that's a business deal. A contract drawn up by a hard-nosed lawyer and with plenty of fine print only makes sure that you will never be able to collect. But if there is no contract in the first place, simply a *promise*—and God's promise at that—you can't break it.

Reflection

Today's world is increasingly governed by legal agreements. They go by many names: contracts, pacts, bonds, and treaties to name a few. Although we might be oblivious to their presence, they govern our everyday life.

For example, we go to the grocery store and buy food with a credit card. At a minimum, this involves three different parties to the transaction: the grocery store, the credit card company, and us. All of these relationships are governed by written agreements and laws, although most of us are completely unaware of the specific terms. They utilize clear and concise language to set out the respective expectations of the parties involved. In our case, the credit card company promises to pay the grocery store. We promise to pay our credit card bill. The grocery store allows us to walk out of the building with the food.

The vast majority of time, everyone does their part, the agreement is completed, and life moves on. In rare cases, someone doesn't fulfill their specified duty, a violation of the agreement occurs, and reparations are made. All in all, it is a smooth operating system that allows us to navigate through the complexities of life. We depend on these agreements, even if we are unaware of them.

Paul spells out how the business deal approach fails when applied to our faith and our relationship with God because God continues to do his part whether or not we do ours. If there is a bargain at stake, God is not depending on us to hold up our end of the deal. God's promises are ironclad and they will be fulfilled. Hard stop. End of story.

Contemplation Questions

1. In what ways do you feel like you have failed to "hold up your end" of the relationship with God?

___

2. What is your perception of how God receives and responds to that?

___

3. If God fulfills his promises regardless if you fulfill yours, how does that impact your faith?

___

> Father God, forgive us for our attempts to bargain with you, or use business-like thinking to manipulate you. Remind us that you, and you alone, will redeem the world. Open our eyes to the fact that you are who you say you are, and you do what you say you will do…and that is more than enough. Humble us in your grace. Strengthen us in your love. Encourage us as we step into this new day.
>
> Amen.

26   Friday

Romans 4:16-18 (MSG)

This is why the fulfillment of God's promise depends entirely on trusting God and his way, and then simply embracing him and what he does. God's promise arrives as pure gift. That's the only way everyone can be sure to get in on it, those who keep the religious traditions *and* those who have never heard of them.

Reflection

Faith is more than just belief. It is trust. Believing is the easy part. We believe that if our feet go out from under us, we will fall. We believe in the physics of the event because we observe a force known as gravity. We may not know let alone be able to explain the rational physical science of it all, but that doesn't stop us from believing.

The same is true of our faith. We believe in all sorts of things that are told to us in scripture that we are unable to comprehend, let alone clarify. How can God be three distinct persons of Father, Son, and Holy Spirit, and yet be one in unity? How can God know all things past, present, and future, and still give us free will? And perhaps most perplexing of all: how can God forgive devastating sins like murder, greed, and infidelity upon the simple act of repentance?

The distinguishing ingredient that transforms mere belief into solid faith is *trust*. It is resting on the promise that if we fall (metaphorically), we will be caught. Trust is the kind of belief that goes above and beyond laws, natural or otherwise. It has the robust expectation that the catching will happen. It is what made Abraham right with God, and through faith in Jesus, puts us right with God too.

Contemplation Questions

1. What areas in life do you find that you trust God completely? What areas do you withhold your trust?

___

2. Identify some of the fears or reasons for withholding your trust.

___

3. How might you take one small step toward trusting God more?

___

> Lord Jesus, as the young father once asked you, "I do believe; help me overcome my unbelief!" Let your affection, forgiveness and gentle guidance transform us into having a solid faith built on trust in you. Humble us in your grace. Strengthen us in your love. Encourage us as we step into this new day.
>
> Amen.

27 — Saturday

Father God, Lord Jesus, and Holy Spirit:

We return to you in full repentance, trusting you with all of our sins and shortcomings.

We remember that you created all of us and knit us together into a history of a family. May we be wise enough to embrace the strength and shed the weakness of it. Remind us that you are our Father, and there is no other like you.

May we pursue good and rightness out of our gratitude for what you have already done for us. May your blessings flow as you direct them. Do not let us succumb to attempts to bargain with you or manipulate you. Remind us that you, and you alone, will redeem the world. Open our eyes to the fact that you are who you say you are, and you do what you say you will do…and that is more than enough.

We do believe. Help us overcome our unbelief. Let your affection, forgiveness, and gentle guidance transform us into having a solid faith built on trust in you.

Humble us in your grace. Strengthen us in your love. Encourage us as we step into this new day.

Amen.

Burguete-Auritz, Spain

Week 5

We have been made right with God because of our faith.
(ERV)

29 — Monday

Romans 5:1-2 (ERV)

We have been made right with God because of our faith. So we have peace with God through our Lord Jesus Christ. Through our faith, Christ has brought us into that blessing of God's grace that we now enjoy. And we are very happy because of the hope we have of sharing God's glory.

Reflection

I've observed a dynamic at work when people acquire fortune, fame, and influence. The more they have, the less accessible they become. This is equally true of the wealthy, celebrities, and politicians. It is a predictable "inverse correlation," meaning that the higher the person is in status, the lower their availability. Ordinary people can't simply insert themselves into the personal circle of the "A-List" individuals of the world, such as billionaires, movie stars, and royalty. This is the way human culture has worked since the beginning of recorded history.

It is no wonder that the previous way of approaching God started to develop elaborate and defined barriers that increasingly kept people away. The longer this perception persisted, the worse the situation seemed to be. Symbolically, this meant God transitioned from traveling with the people in a portable tabernacle into the penthouse of an elaborate stone temple. From the establishment's viewpoint, God's status was perceived to be so high that accessibility to the common person was determined to be nearly impossible. It was unseemly to think that average people could just insert themselves into the orbit of the Creator of the Universe. Enter Jesus.

It is no mistake that Jesus was from a backwater province of a third-world kingdom that was under the subjugation of the world's largest empire. Jesus was the most *anti* "A-List" personality imaginable. It also sheds light on why he consistently ducked large adoring crowds and deflected attention away from himself. He wanted to remain accessible to every person, but especially to the person who was on the opposite end of the inverse correlation equation–people who completely lacked any touch of fortune, fame, and influence. The poor. The forgotten. The powerless. The work of Jesus was to throw *open* the doors of access to God and throw *out* any concept of relegation due to status and standing. Our excuse of unworthiness will never be an acceptable one for approaching God. We all come into the presence, grace, and love of God on equal footing. We all have "A-List" privileges to Jesus.

Contemplation Questions

1. How available and accessible is God to you? How available and accessible are you to God?

   _____
   _____
   _____
   _____

2. Reflect on your self-worth and the impact on your relationship to God. Does it make God feel closer or further away?

   _____
   _____
   _____
   _____

3. What could you do to have God feel one step closer?

   _____
   _____
   _____
   _____

> Heavenly Father, forgive us for when we excuse ourselves from your presence because we tell ourselves we are not worthy. Remind us that you will never, ever turn us away because of reputation or situation. Instill in us the realization that we are your beloved children. Reclaim us in your grace. Rebuild us in your love. Reform us into your perfect plan as we step into this new day.
>
> Amen.

30   Tuesday

Romans 5:3-5 (NIV)

Not only so, but we also glory in our sufferings, because we know that suffering produces perseverance; perseverance, character; and character, hope. And hope does not put us to shame, because God's love has been poured out into our hearts through the Holy Spirit, who has been given to us.

Reflection

I am fascinated by the amazing network of organs in the human body known as muscles. Attached to our bones, they are the source of all bodily movement and consist of about 50% of our total body weight. They range in size from smallest (located in the middle ear), to the largest (our gluteus maximus), to the most active (our eye muscles) to the most unique (our tongue, which is the only one not connected on both ends to a bone).

Even after we mature, most muscles have the capability to grow even stronger. However, that only happens when the muscle endures some degree of suffering and injury. This is because, as the muscle repairs itself, it gets bigger and tougher to avoid the injury from happening again. Thus, the physical pain resulting from working our muscles is not always a bad thing, or as General Lewis "Chesty" Puller famously said, "Pain is weakness leaving the body."

Trouble and suffering have the same effect on our "spiritual muscles" of faith. While they are painful to experience, they usually turn out to be the most formative moments in our development. The critical difference is knowing *how* to approach, endure, and exit the experience. And, at the same time, we must have confidence that those experiences will be redeemed by God for our own benefit. It will produce in us the strong fibers of faith, such as resilience, integrity, and trust.

Contemplation Questions

1. Can you identify recent or current suffering and how might it be connected to your faith?

_____

_____

_____

_____

2. Does God feel far during these times? If so, what practices might draw him closer?

_____

_____

_____

_____

3. How might God be redeeming these experiences to increase your faith?

_____

_____

_____

_____

> Lord Jesus, reside with us in our suffering. Remind us that we always should lean into you, but especially in the moments and seasons when we feel downtrodden and cast aside. If we are willing, you will redeem those moments for our benefit and for your glory. Reclaim us in your grace. Rebuild us in your love. Reform us into your perfect plan as we step into this new day.
>
> Amen.

31   Wednesday

Romans 5:6-8 (NIV)

You see, at just the right time, when we were still powerless, Christ died for the ungodly. Very rarely will anyone die for a righteous person, though for a good person someone might possibly dare to die. But God demonstrates his own love for us in this: While we were still sinners, Christ died for us.

Reflection

Sacrifice is a noble word. It is an action verb. It means to suffer loss or give up something, usually for an ideal, belief, or greater good. We celebrate and admire acts of sacrifice. For example, our country celebrates Memorial Day in remembrance of the men and women who died while serving in a branch of the military. We plant flags and flowers on their graves, attend parades, and are grateful for what "sacrifice" has provided to our nation.

Yet, it is increasingly hard for us to think and act in terms of sacrifice when we are surrounded by a culture that values accumulation of material things, status, and wealth. Is it possible that our appreciation and respect for acts of sacrifice cover-up our own fear and shame? Perhaps we are secretly afraid that if called upon, we couldn't summon the courage to do the same thing, since our self-interest is not only about our own survival but also focused on "getting ahead."

This is what makes the sacrifice of Jesus so difficult to fully understand. That he left the privilege of heaven to join us here in the dirt of the earth is hard enough to grasp, let alone that he then suffered through a horrible crucifixion to atone for our crimes. To be sure, we're elated that he did it for us. But do we stop and recognize that he also did it for the person we would gladly see burn in hell? This is the unfathomable depth of Jesus' love. It is unconditional. No fine print or disclaimers disqualify any person from receiving it. It is sacrifice in the truest sense of the word.

Contemplation Questions

1. Where in your life have you noticed that you were unwilling to share or give up something for the benefit of someone else?

   _____

   _____

   _____

   _____

2. Jesus repeatedly says that selflessness, sacrifice, and suffering are the way of the Kingdom. Reflect on the underlying reasons why that is necessary.

   _____

   _____

   _____

   _____

3. Where might you experience God if he invited you into a time of sacrifice and suffering?

   _____

   _____

   _____

   _____

> Lord Jesus, you have sacrificed your life on a cross for every person who has lived, is living, or will ever live. It is an astounding act of selflessness. Since we now have nothing to fear, may it inspire us to think, speak, and act sacrificially. Give us the courage to do it only for your glory. Reclaim us in your grace. Rebuild us in your love. Reform us into your perfect plan as we step into this new day.
>
> Amen.

32 — Thursday

Romans 5:9-11 (MSG)

Now that we are set right with God by means of this sacrificial death, the consummate blood sacrifice, there is no longer a question of being at odds with God in any way… Now that we have actually received this amazing friendship with God, we are no longer content to simply say it in plodding prose. We sing and shout our praises to God through Jesus, the Messiah!

Reflection

The sacrifice of Jesus for every person's sins, including ours, is mind boggling. But the "work" that it accomplishes is even more so. Theologically, it is known as *justification*. We are justified in front of God because of what Jesus has done for us. Sadly, the fullness of the blessing is a gift that not many of us appreciate.

When we are justified by Jesus' work on the cross, it is far more than forgiveness. It expunges and obliterates the record of our sins, past, present, and future. It does away with the notion that God maintains a permanent file of failures with our name on it even after we are forgiven. Justification means we are treated as if we had never sinned.

The Psalmist captures a visual of justification when he writes, "as far as the east is from the west, so far has he removed our transgressions from us" (NIV Psalm 103:12). To fully understand this image, we must remember that if we travel north, at some point we will reach the north pole and have no choice but to travel south. However, when traveling east, we can go in that direction forever and never be forced to turn back west. In other words, through justification, God separates us from our sins by the measure of infinitude. We are cleansed completely, and no trace of our transgressions is left within us. We are restored to our right relationship with our Father.

Contemplation Questions

1. What sins, failures, and hurts are you still carrying within you?

___

2. Consider some reasons why it is so important to God to forgive our sins.

___

3. What invitations and possibilities open to you with the realization that God has literally forgotten your past transgressions and failures?

___

> Lord Jesus, pardon our mindset that we are never truly free from our sins, as if they are only forgiven but not forgotten. Remind us that your sacrifice returns us to our original position of beloved child of the Father, free of transgressions. Reclaim us in your grace. Rebuild us in your love. Reform us into your perfect plan as we step into this new day.
>
> Amen.

33 — Friday

Romans 5:12-14 (MSG)

You know the story of how Adam landed us in the dilemma we're in—first sin, then death, and no one exempt from either sin or death…But Adam, who got us into this, also points ahead to the One who will get us out of it.

Reflection

Our bodies carry within us a lot of history of our family of origin. Physically, genetic traits are handed down from one generation to the next. Similarly, patterns of thought and behavior are embedded in neural pathways of our brains, reflecting how we were raised.

The same is true for our *original* sin, which can trace back to the first human: Adam. As the first in humanity, Adam enjoyed a covenantal relationship with God. As our earthly forefather, those blessings were expected to flow through mankind all the way until it reached us. Unfortunately, the reverse is equally true. The consequence of Adam's disobedience attached itself to us as well. We cannot escape our spiritual DNA. Left as is, there would be no hope for us. No thanks to Adam, there is nothing we could do to get us out of our predicament.

But what Adam left destroyed, Jesus came to restore, which is why he is frequently referred to as the "Second Adam." It explains why Jesus had to be fully human, because he too is part of our family of origin. He had to reset the broken genetic mutation of our sin. And because he did this by his sacrifice on the cross, we are made right with God.

Contemplation Questions

1. What sins and patterns of unhealthy behavior do you notice in your family of origin?

   _____
   _____
   _____
   _____

2. How have the sins and unhealthy behaviors of your family impacted or influenced your own sense of self?

   _____
   _____
   _____
   _____

3. How might Jesus best lead you to the fullness of who he created you to be?

   _____
   _____
   _____
   _____

> Heavenly Father, thank you for the healing of our brokenness you have given us in your son Jesus. He did what we could never do, restore our relationship with you. May we never take that beautiful gift for granted. Reclaim us in your grace. Rebuild us in your love. Reform us into your perfect plan as we step into this new day.
>
> Amen.

34 — Saturday

Heavenly Father, Lord Jesus, and Holy Spirit:

Forgive us for when we excuse ourselves from your presence because we tell ourselves we are not worthy. Remind us that you will never, ever turn us away because of reputation or situation.

Instill in us the realization that we are your beloved children, and that your sacrifice returns us to our original position of beloved child of the Father, free of transgressions.

In our times of pain and suffering, remind us that we always should lean into you. Because of your sacrifice, we have nothing to fear. Give us eyes to detect the redemption that comes out of those times so that we may be encouraged, and your name receives glory.

Give us courage to think, speak, and act sacrificially because our relationship has been restored. May we never take that beautiful gift for granted.

Reclaim us in your grace. Rebuild us in your love. Reform us into your perfect plan as we step into this new day.

Amen.

Pyrenees Mountains, France

Week 6

If death got the upper hand through one man's wrongdoing...
(MSG)

36 Monday

Romans 5:15-17 (MSG)

If death got the upper hand through one man's wrongdoing, can you imagine the breathtaking recovery life makes, absolute life, in those who grasp with both hands this wildly extravagant life-gift, this grand setting-everything-right, that the one man Jesus Christ provides?

Reflection

Devastating wildfires frequently begin with a small, unattended flame. It doesn't take long for a small, insignificant spark to grow into a huge inferno consuming everything in its path. Even if firefighters have the luxury of committing vast resources to combat it, the most common strategy is to contain it rather than extinguish it.

The same is true for our sins. We can trace the source of our sins back to Adam's first act of disobedience, but that single sin has long since exploded into a worldwide conflagration. Even at our best, the most we can hope to accomplish through our own efforts is to contain them and limit the wake of the destruction they leave behind.

This is why Christ's atoning grace is infinitely larger than Adam's original sin. In fact, to compare the two would be an affront to Jesus' sacrifice. His love is so strong that it does more than contain the sin, it extinguishes it.

Contemplation Questions

1. Can you detect any fear, anxiety, or shame that keeps you from seeking forgiveness?

   _____
   _____
   _____
   _____
   _____

2. Wildfires leave behind a wake of destruction. What damage do you see from your sins?

   _____
   _____
   _____
   _____
   _____

3. How do you allow Jesus' forgiveness to confront your own sins and brokenness?

   _____
   _____
   _____
   _____
   _____

Lord Jesus, your forgiveness covers not only our sins, but the sins of the entire world. Remind us that your comfort will chase away our fear and anxiety. Recover us through your grace. Restore us in your love. Reveal your presence among us as we step into this new day.

Amen.

37

Tuesday

Romans 5:18-21 (MSG)

All that passing laws against sin did was produce more lawbreakers. But sin didn't, and doesn't, have a chance in competition with the aggressive forgiveness we call *grace*. When it's sin versus grace, grace wins hands down. All sin can do is threaten us with death, and that's the end of it. Grace, because God is putting everything together again through the Messiah, invites us into life—a life that goes on and on and on, world without end.

Reflection

Mirrors have a sneaky way of causing an impulsive reaction within us. Few of us can walk by one without stealing a glance at our own reflection. We want to know how we look. Unfortunately, we also have to accept what we see looking back at us. The old saying that "a mirror never lies" holds true because the rules of physics do not include any elements of politeness or gentleness in producing the reflection. It is just stone-cold natural law at work, and what we see is what exists.

God's law works in the same way as a mirror, except, instead of showing our physical selves, it reveals our moral and ethical selves. Like the physical mirror, the reflection we receive is equally direct and unfiltered. It doesn't lie to us. But the purpose of God's law is not to be harsh or cruel. Rather, it is there to reveal the brutal extent to which we are broken. As a result, unlike our fascination with physical mirrors, most of us diligently avoid peeking at the reflection given by God's law because the truth of the image we encounter is too tough to reconcile with our self-perception.

Thankfully, God gives us a third mirror in the person of Jesus. The reflective property of this mirror is known as "grace." It shows the fullness of who God created us to be. It corrects the distortions created by our sins. But more importantly, it invites us to turn away from our obsession with the mirror, and toward the love and life we have in God.

Contemplation Questions

1. How willing are you to look into the "mirror" of your inner self?

_____

_____

_____

_____

2. What do you see reflected back to you? Is your reflection distorted or clear?

_____

_____

_____

_____

3. What would the fullness of who God created you to be look like?

_____

_____

_____

_____

> Heavenly Father, we are created in your image, but forgive us when we live with a false image of our own making. Deflate our pride. Chase away our self-loathing. Give us eyes to see ourselves how you see us: as beloved children in need of a savior. Recover us through your grace. Restore us in your love. Reveal your presence among us as we step into this new day.
>
> Amen.

38 — Wednesday

Romans 6:1-5 (MSG)

So what do we do? Keep on sinning so God can keep on forgiving? I should hope not! If we've left the country where sin is sovereign, how can we still live in our old house there? Or didn't you realize we packed up and left there for good? That is what happened in baptism. When we went under the water, we left the old country of sin behind; when we came up out of the water, we entered into the new country of grace—a new life in a new land!

Reflection

If the grace of Jesus is the best thing in the world, then why not load up on it as much as possible? Is it really possible to have too much of a good thing? The answer lies in the descriptor "too much." By definition, too much of anything is exactly that: excessive and gluttonous. To invoke grace means we are turning away from sin. To continually sin and just rely on forgiveness empties grace of all meaning. It reduces it to nothing more than an unhealthy, if not destructive, coping mechanism.

Grace is a gift, not a license. To confuse the first with the second is to have a profound misunderstanding of the Gospel message. Having a license means we've been given permission by a qualified authority to do something that would otherwise be forbidden. Why would Jesus proactively permit us to do that which is hurtful, harmful, and/or unhealthy? On the contrary, he is always seeking to transform us into God's image. He is not going to advocate for something that causes our own disfigurement.

When we properly see grace as a gift, we recognize it for what it truly is: something to be received with gratitude and humility. For sure it is a life-giving and life-changing experience, but so is being rescued from a burning building or saved from drowning; neither of which we'd seek to repeat on a regular basis. Grace is a God-given pardon we are privileged to use, but not to abuse.

Contemplation Questions

1. How often do you contemplate the generosity and magnanimity of God's grace?

_____
_____
_____
_____

2. Do you find that you depend on grace to excuse a sin before you actually commit it?

_____
_____
_____
_____

3. Where do you find God in the midst of that decision?

_____
_____
_____
_____

> Lord Jesus, forgive us for our mistreatment and abuse of your gift of grace. The incomparable, soul-saving action that you offer us with no strings attached. Lord, who are we that you would do this for us? May our attitude and actions going forward reflect our gratefulness as you continually transform us into who we're meant to be. Recover us through your grace. Restore us in your love. Reveal your presence among us as we step into this new day.
>
> Amen.

39   Thursday

Romans 6:6-11 (MSG)

When Jesus died, he took sin down with him, but alive he brings God down to us. From now on, think of it this way: Sin speaks a dead language that means nothing to you; God speaks your mother tongue, and you hang on every word. You are dead to sin and alive to God. That's what Jesus did.

Reflection

In the opening sentences of the book of Romans, Paul rightly points out that God's creation has an almost inexhaustible supply of clues and examples of God's presence and work in the world. We are "without excuse" for knowing God because the evidence is all around us.

This is also true for what it means to be "dead to our sins and alive in Christ" (NIV). The caterpillar is one stunning example of metamorphosis that speaks to this kind of change. After living a span of time in that form, it stops eating, hangs upside down from a twig, and spins itself into a protective cocoon. Inside the cocoon, the caterpillar undergoes a radical transformation. The process is so thorough that if we were to open the cocoon at the right time, all we would find is a primordial goo that is neither caterpillar nor butterfly. But when the time is right, a fully structured butterfly emerges.

This natural process of the butterfly points to a higher, supernatural process when we submit our lives to the cleansing and transforming change of grace in Christ. It is not easily understood, let alone explained. However, we do know that it is radical. A spiritual condition within us is irretrievably changed and we emerge completely different from our previous form.

Contemplation Questions

1. Do you discern invitations from God to change who you are?

_____

_____

_____

_____

2. What do those invitations look like?

_____

_____

_____

_____

3. How are you responding to those invitations?

_____

_____

_____

_____

> Holy Spirit, we know that we are transformed through grace, even though we can't see it or fully understand it. Give us the wisdom to look for it, and the patience to let it happen. Recover us through your grace. Restore us in your love. Reveal your presence among us as we step into this new day.
>
> Amen.

40 Friday

Romans 6:12-14 (ERV)

But don't let sin control your life here on earth. You must not be ruled by the things your sinful self makes you want to do. Don't offer the parts of your body to serve sin. Don't use your bodies to do evil, but offer yourselves to God, as people who have died and now live. Offer the parts of your body to God to be used for doing good. Sin will not be your master, because you are not under law. You now live under God's grace.

Reflection

It is firmly established that a life in unrepentant sin is equal to death. If we imagine that our sinful state is like we are treading water in the middle of the ocean with no dry land in sight, we get a sense of our hopeless situation. We might be able to keep our head above the waves for an incredibly long time, but we will not thrive. Eventually, we will drown.

Now imagine we are rescued by a ship specifically designed for the purpose. The crew scoops us out of the water and deposits us safely on deck. As thankful as we would be in the moment, at some point later, many of us are going to jump back into the predicament we were just liberated from. As foolish as that appears, it is the same kind of foolishness as continuing in our old sinful ways.

We should never underestimate the siren song of sin and the overwhelming tidal pull it has on our will power. It is always beckoning us back into the water. But as we engage in that struggle, we should recognize that the question is no longer about whether or not we will drown. The justifying power of Jesus' grace will not allow that to happen. Rather, the question is if we want to live a life tossed about in an ocean of devastation and depravity. If we don't, then the only way it happens is if we stop diving back into it.

Contemplation Questions

1. In nautical terms, the weather conditions of the ocean are called the "sea state." What is the "sea state" of your life right now? Is it stormy or calm?

_____

_____

_____

_____

2. Can you identify times when you jumped back in the water? What was your rationale?

_____

_____

_____

_____

3. What are some strategies you could develop for staying on the boat?

_____

_____

_____

_____

> Jesus, you have rescued us from drowning in our sins. Forgive us for our stubborn habit of going back to them. Open our eyes to the reality that life in you frees us from a life of chaos and volatility. Let us accept the invitation of peace that comes patterning our ways after yours. Recover us through your grace. Restore us in your love. Reveal your presence among us as we step into this new day.
>
> Amen.

41 — Saturday

Heavenly Father, Lord Jesus, and Holy Spirit:

We have traveled another week with you. In our time, we pray that your transforming work continues in us.

As we walked with you, we were reminded that your forgiveness covers not only our sins, but the sins of the entire world. Your love extends to all people because we are created in your image.

We learned that we live within a false image of our own making. The view of our true self is distorted. We ask that you deflate our pride and chase away our self-loathing. Give us eyes to see ourselves how you see us: as beloved children in need of a savior.

Forgive us for our mistreatment and abuse of your gift of grace—the incomparable, soul-saving action that you offer us with no strings attached. Who are we, that you would do this for us? May our attitude and actions going forward reflect our gratefulness as you continually transform us into who we were meant to be, even though there are long stretches where we can't see it or fully understand it. Give us the wisdom to search for it, and the patience to let it happen.

Recover us through your grace. Restore us in your love. Reveal your presence among us as we step into this new day

Amen.

Week 6

Villamayor del Rio, Spain

Week 7

You know well enough from your own experience...
(MSG)

43 Monday

Romans 6:15-19 (MSG)

You know well enough from your own experience that there are some acts of so-called freedom that destroy freedom. Offer yourselves to sin, for instance, and it's your last free act. But offer yourselves to the ways of God and the freedom never quits. All your lives you've let sin tell you what to do. But thank God you've started listening to a new master, one whose commands set you free to live openly in *his* freedom!

Reflection

God could have easily created us as automatons—no better than robots who follow pre-established programming. But from the beginning, he created us in his image, and with it came the freedom to obey or disobey. We see this in the story of Adam and Eve.

As we consider all the decisions and choices we make throughout life, we do so weighing external factors, such as potential rewards and consequences, as well as satisfying our own needs and the needs of others. More importantly, as we continually make these determinations, we need to recognize that they are largely self-motivated. In theology it is known as "free will." It is a God-given gift of autonomy.

This independence to make choices and to act of our own will is a beautiful but fearsome privilege. We can do good, or we can do evil. It can lead to blessing, or it can court disaster. However, because of the power and influence of sin, we are ill-equipped to handle it on our own. Unchecked, it is no better than chaos. It is why we need to accept Jesus' invitation to live a life that he himself has patterned for us. He doesn't simply tell us; he shows us. And from it, we find healthy boundaries for our free will that lead to fulfillment, significance, and connectedness.

Contemplation Questions

1. How valuable or important is your free will to you?

___

2. Where has your freedom to choose enhanced your life? Where has it hurt it?

___

3. When and how do you detect God's presence when you are making life choices?

___

> Heavenly Father, thank you for trusting us with a gift of self-determination in daily life. Yet, forgive us when we abuse and misuse that freedom in ways that lead to poor, harsh, or dangerous decisions. We recognize that left to our own devices, we would wander the desert forever. Guide us back to you and your ways. Excuse us in your grace. Empower us in your love. Enlighten us with your wisdom. Lead us in the way we should go as we step into this new day.
>
> Amen.

44 — Tuesday

Romans 6:20-23 (MSG)

But now that you've found you don't have to listen to sin tell you what to do, and have discovered the delight of listening to God telling you, what a surprise! A whole, healed, put-together life right now, with more and more of life on the way! Work hard for sin your whole life and your pension is death. But God's gift is *real life*, eternal life, delivered by Jesus, our Master.

Reflection

When a judge or jury hands down a "not guilty" verdict, the defendant in the trial is discharged from any and all impending penalties connected to that specific crime. At that moment, the defendant's future—at least as it relates to the crime—is decided.

The same is true when we receive the saving grace of Jesus. In that moment, we are made right before God from that point forward into eternity. The theological term for it is *justification*. It is a one-time event because God has dealt with the guilty sentence that accompanies our sin. It is abolished and our criminal record is expunged. (See devotional #32 covering Romans 5:9-11.)

But just as being discharged with a "not guilty" verdict by a judge or jury does not deal with the residual behaviors that led to being charged with the crime in the first place, justification does not relieve us from our continual desire to engage in sin. Addressing that problem requires us to engage in the process of *sanctification*—or setting ourselves apart. We continue to seek Jesus even after he has declared us "not guilty" because he will lead us in ways that bring blessing and not adversity.

Contemplation Questions

1. If God could physically hand you an official written declaration of "not guilty" that you could frame and hang on a wall to look at every day, what might change in how you live your life?

___

___

___

___

2. Can you identify the "residual behaviors" of sin that persist in your life? Can you detect the impact they have? Are they positive or negative?

___

___

___

___

3. How might pursuing "sanctification" help address those residual behaviors? Where do you think God would reveal himself in those efforts?

___

___

___

___

> Lord Jesus, you gave your life for ours. In that moment, we were forgiven and set free of our sins. Yet, forgive us for all the times we return to them as if your sacrifice had no meaning or effect. Lead us in the way of sanctification. Excuse us in your grace. Empower us in your love. Enlighten us with your wisdom. Lead us in the way we should go as we step into this new day.
>
> Amen.

45

Wednesday

Romans 7:1-6 (ERV)

In the past the law held us as prisoners, but our old selves died, and we were made free from the law. So now we serve God in a new way, not in the old way, with the written rules. Now we serve God in the new way, with the Spirit.

Reflection

Our ongoing liaison with sin is like a toxic relationship. There is an emotional and irrational attachment that keeps us trapped in its grip. We resort to all manner of justifying and explaining it away. The purpose of God's law is simply to make clear what we try so hard to disguise.

As a result of our perceived inability to escape, we feel guilt, become jaded, and/or simply ignore the inevitable outcomes from a continued slavery to sin. Deep down, we know we should abandon it, but somehow, we can't summon the courage or the fortitude. It is a vicious cycle, which is why it is so toxic.

The starting point for escaping the toxicity is always the grace of Jesus. His forgiveness allows us to forgive ourselves. His love allows us to respect ourselves. His redemption allows us to start anew. These three core truths destroy the power of sin over our lives. More importantly, it leads us into a healthy and sustaining relationship with him.

Contemplation Questions

1. Are you able to detect the continuing sins in your life? Would you describe any of them as "toxic"? Why or why not?

2. What emotions do you detect within yourself that flow from those continuing sins? Are there elements of guilt, anger, or resentment?

3. Identify one step you could take to liberate yourself from the continuing pattern. What do you need to do in order to implement that step?

Lord Jesus, we ask for your grace, love, and redemption. Even if we have asked for these before, we know you will not turn us away when we humbly ask again. Destroy sin's toxic grip. Invite us into a wholesome bond with you. Excuse us in your grace. Empower us in your love. Enlighten us with your wisdom. Lead us in the way of sanctification and direct us in the way we should go as we step into this new day.

Amen.

46 — Thursday

Romans 7:7 (MSG)

The law code had a perfectly legitimate function. Without its clear guidelines for right and wrong, moral behavior would be mostly guesswork. Apart from the succinct, surgical command, "You shall not covet," I could have dressed covetousness up to look like a virtue and ruined my life with it.

Reflection

Rules and regulations are not an end unto themselves. They are always created to express an underlying value. Invariably, the expression of those values boil down to either directing or limiting human actions. As Martin Luther King, Jr. famously said, "Morality cannot be legislated, but behavior can be regulated. Judicial decrees may not change the heart, but they can restrain the heartless."

This is true for "God's Law" as well. God intended it as something to abide in—not to be worshiped. When pursuit of that law zealously supersedes the underlying value, God's love, grace, and justice are lost. It results in reducing God's law from something sacred into a simple ordinance that is to be blindly followed.

Jesus changed the prevailing view on the law. He repeatedly quoted the prophet Hosea in saying, "Go learn what this means: 'I desire mercy, not sacrifice.'" He also told us he didn't abolish the law, but to the contrary, fulfilled it. This means that Jesus *is* the expression of the underlying value for the law, and therefore the rules and regulations must be interpreted and obeyed through him.

Contemplation Questions

1. How would you characterize the way you follow or obey rules?

   _____

   _____

   _____

   _____

2. When you encounter a rule or law, do you try to detect the underlying value(s)? How might knowing and understanding the underlying value impact your compliance?

   _____

   _____

   _____

   _____

3. Which "rules" found in scripture do you pattern your life after? How many of them are you able to identify? Can you articulate the value of those "rules" and what God might be seeking through them? Where might God be inviting you into a healthier life with him through rules?

   _____

   _____

   _____

   _____

> Jesus, forgive us when we are only interested in knowing the rules instead of knowing you. When we only want to follow the regulations instead of following you. Lord, correct us when our obedience is misdirected. Excuse us in your grace. Empower us in your love. Enlighten us with your wisdom. Lead us in the way we should go as we step into this new day.
>
> Amen.

47 Friday

Romans 7:8-12 (MSG)

The law code started out as an excellent piece of work. What happened, though, was that sin found a way to pervert the command into a temptation, making a piece of "forbidden fruit" out of it. The law code, instead of being used to guide me, was used to seduce me.

Reflection

When we think of the word "sin," typically we associate it with emotions of guilt and shame. While those emotions have an important function in changing our behavior, there is more to the concept of sin than just making us feel bad. The Greek word for sin is *hamartia*. The source of the word comes from a Greek verb *hamartanein*, which means "to miss the mark." It calls to mind the image of an archer who doesn't hit the intended target.

To grasp a fuller understanding of what is being communicated, imagine all our words and actions as metaphorical "arrows" being launched from a bow. As archers, we should care about the destination of every one of our arrows that finds flight because experience has taught us that some, and perhaps many, miss the mark. We should recognize that the consequence of missing the mark always results in harm—to God, to others, and to us.

While the grace of Jesus will erase the eternal consequences of those misdirected arrows, it should also serve as a call to become better archers. It is a call to focus on the right target, give attention to our posture and technique, and choose which arrows to use, and which ones should remain in the quiver.

Contemplation Questions

1. Do we recognize the damage caused by our "sin arrows" that "miss the mark?" What emotions do we experience when we cause that damage?

2. In what ways does God lead us to recovery from the injury and restoration of the damage? Are we willing to follow that lead? Why or why not?

3. What might we do to become better "archers" in word and deed?

> Father God, forgive us for our wayward arrows that inflict pain, suffering, and damage to others, to ourselves, and to you. Lead us in the steps we need to take to bring about healing and restoration. Excuse us in your grace. Empower us in your love. Enlighten us with your wisdom. Invite us to become better examples of your grace, love, and peace.
>
> Amen.

48 — Saturday

Father, Son, and Holy Spirit:

We praise you for how wonderfully we are made. We thank you for trusting us with a gift of self-determination in daily life. Yet, forgive us when we abuse and misuse that freedom. When we only are interested in knowing the rules instead of knowing you. We recognize that left to our own devices, we would wander the desert forever.

Lord Jesus, you gave your life for ours. In that moment, we were forgiven and set free of our sins. But forgive us for our continual wandering back and forth between basking in your love and engaging in heartless sin. We act as if your sacrifice had no meaning. We struggle to know you because we don't even know ourselves.

We ask for your grace, love, and redemption. Even if we have asked for these before, we know you will not turn us away when we humbly ask again. Destroy sin's toxic grip.

Let this be the day where we once again lay our life at your feet. Lead us in the way of sanctification. Invite us into a wholesome bond with you. Guide us back to you and your ways.

Excuse us in your grace. Empower us in your love. Enlighten us with your wisdom. Lead us in the way we should go as we step into this new day.

Amen.

Week 7

Zabaldica, Spain

Week 8

I don't understand why I act the way I do.
(ERV)

50 Monday

Romans 7:13-16 (ERV)

I don't understand why I act the way I do. I don't do the good I want to do, and I do the evil I hate. And if I don't want to do what I do, that means I agree that the law is good. But I am not really the one doing the evil. It is sin living in me that does it.

Reflection

We, as individual humans, are incredibly complex and mysterious creations of God. We have tangible bodies, and yet experience intangible thoughts and emotions. We recognize physical reality, and yet have a sense of the spiritual. We understand ourselves as both real and ethereal.

All these reveal a different, yet intertwined, facet of our *being*. So who we are, how we think, and what we feel is not easily explained, let alone solved. The paradox of how we are beautifully made in God's image, and yet faulty due to our sin is beyond our grasp. In sum, we are a mystery to ourselves, and it is reflected in the confusing and contradictory ways we live our lives.

But God has not left us adrift in bewilderment. Stepping into our mysterious selves, our unique blend of splendor and repulsiveness, comes the grace of Jesus. His grace too is full of irony. It brings with it the sharp edge of truth, but also the healing power of love. It establishes strong boundaries of behavior, but also advocates for mercy. Thankfully, his grace meets us where it finds us, but it doesn't leave us there.

Contemplation Questions

1. What about the way you were created makes God smile? Where do you detect God's beautiful handiwork?

___

2. What truths about ourselves do we hide from others, or ignore ourselves?

___

3. In what ways might God be inviting you into the fullness of who he created you to be?

___

> Lord, we praise you for how wonderfully we are made. But forgive us for our continual wandering back and forth between basking in your love and engaging in heartless sin. We struggle to know you because we don't even know ourselves. Let this be the day where we once again lay our life at your feet. Excuse us in your grace. Empower us in your love. Enlighten us with your wisdom. Lead us in the way we should go as we step into this new day.
>
> Amen.

51 Tuesday

Romans 7:17-23 (MSG)

For if I know the law but still can't keep it, and if the power of sin within me keeps sabotaging my best intentions, I obviously need help! I realize that I don't have what it takes. I can will it, but I can't *do* it. I decide to do good, but I don't *really* do it; I decide not to do bad, but then I do it anyway. My decisions, such as they are, don't result in actions. Something has gone wrong deep within me and gets the better of me every time.

Reflection

The NIV translation of today's scripture might have a more familiar ring to some: "For I do not do the good I want to do, but the evil I do not want to do—this I keep on doing." But no matter what translation we use, *every* Christian should resonate with this observation from Paul. Even though the Holy Spirit resides within us, sin has not given up its grip on us. Unfortunately, that reality can cause us to question whether we really submitted ourselves to Christ and received his grace.

While Paul is being transparent in his own struggle, he is also laying the groundwork to communicate a new perspective on our present predicament. Our current circumstance is that we are caught up in the war between two realms. In Jesus, God has begun the inbreaking of his kingdom into our broken world. However, the battle is not over. The D-Day invasion has happened, but evil has not surrendered. Full victory is assured, but the liberation that comes with it is still in the future. Theologically, it is often referred to as "the already, but not yet."

It is a struggle to live in the territory of "the already, but not yet." Life is not easy when we are caught up in the crossfire of this war. Like any good citizen who seeks deliverance from the evil occupiers of our land, we think and act in ways that help the cause of God. We practice grace, we sacrifice for others, we love our neighbors. But just as often, we revert to our old ways of selfishness, greed, and hate. Sometimes it is due to simple inattentiveness. Other times we simply give in and justify it in the name of survival.

What should we do amid this war where we endlessly switch between obedience and rebellion? Perhaps we need reminding of the attributes of God. Our salvation isn't up for grabs because sin and death have already been defeated. We have the freedom to choose obedience, but we are not forced into it. We can participate in the cause of Christ, but it is not demanded. Satan is the one that uses coercion, not the Holy Spirit. Once we recognize this reality, we can better receive the invitation to rest in Jesus. We can take up the cause of God in this war because we know it will not result in our death, but life to the fullest.

Contemplation Questions

1. What joys do you experience in the "already, but not yet" of God's coming kingdom? What are the frustrations? How do the two balance out against each other?

_____

_____

_____

_____

2. What specific attributes of God would be helpful for you to remember today? Have you prayed for those attributes to reveal themselves to you?

_____

_____

_____

_____

3. What practices of obedience could you observe today that would be helpful to your faith?

_____

_____

_____

_____

> Holy Spirit, we ask for forgiveness. Although we long for the fullness of the "Kingdom come" to earth, we act in favor of evil. You have made us new, but we continually revert to our old ways. Give us your peace and remind us that we are safe. Renew the invitation to participate with you in the cause of good and right. Humble us in your grace. Strengthen us in your love. Encourage us as we step into this new day.
>
> Amen.

52 Wednesday

Romans 7:24-25 (ERV)

What a miserable person I am! Who will save me from this body that brings me death? I thank God for his salvation through Jesus Christ our Lord!

Reflection

Paul's words bring an inward battle out into the light. He did not want it to be a secret struggle, because it is only in darkness that evil can do its work. Thus, by example, he openly admits his own weaknesses and inadequacies. It is a vivid and vicarious portrayal of our broken status.

Paul recognized that within the ongoing tug-of-war between our desire to pursue obedience and our inclination to embrace rebellion, the tension will eventually wear us out. It highlights the danger of becoming overly focused on that continuing conflict, because hopelessness will inevitably creep in. Then, as a result, we will begin to fall into the old trap of thinking that our salvation rests on our own shoulders.

This is not to say that we are not responsible for our own actions. We must be vigilant in resisting the temptation of sin. But that struggle is not the sole focus of our faith. Rather, it should always redirect us toward our dependency on the grace of Jesus. It must continually remind us of the resiliency of his enduring love. In short, it makes us aware that we are not in this battle alone.

Contemplation Questions

1. In what ways might your efforts at "obedience" result in you feeling like you are wearing out your faith?

   _____
   _____
   _____
   _____

2. Where do you detect the presence of God in the midst of this experience?

   _____
   _____
   _____
   _____

3. How could God remind you of his enduring love and care?

   _____
   _____
   _____
   _____

> Lord Jesus, we are, indeed, at the end of our rope. We have good intentions but they dissolve into harmful actions. We repeat over and over our sins, and your forgiveness often feels far away. Return our attention to you. Remind us of your love. Fill us with your grace. Inspire us to walk in the way you would have us go.
>
> Amen.

53   Thursday

Romans 8:1-4 (MSG)

God went for the jugular when he sent his own Son. He didn't deal with the problem as something remote and unimportant. In his Son, Jesus, he personally took on the human condition, entered the disordered mess of struggling humanity in order to set it right once and for all. The law code, weakened as it always was by fractured human nature, could never have done that.

Reflection

The NIV translation of the opening of Chapter 8 might strike us as more familiar: "There is, therefore, now no condemnation for those who are in Christ Jesus." Whatever translation we use, verse 1 should be permanently etched into our minds as a marching order for faith. Through the grace of Jesus, we are made right with God. In that sacred and momentous instance, we receive the triple blessing of loving acceptance, unconditional immunity, and permanent security. It will never be revoked. Ever.

Such is the unimaginable and insurmountable power of Jesus' forgiveness. But there is more. Much more. Because in the same moment of justification, we also receive the Holy Spirit. In receiving the Spirit, we embark on a lifelong journey with God's presence dwelling in us, also known as *sanctification*.

To engage in sanctification only requires that we allow the Spirit to lead us. Since the Spirit is never coercive, our role is to cultivate a posture that tunes into that leading. God's Word serves as guide markers, leading us towards "what the Spirit is doing in us."

Contemplation Questions

1. In what ways are you comforted and encouraged by the fact that Jesus "conquered" the consequence of sin? How might you live into that today?

_____
_____
_____
_____

2. How do you make time and space to receive the presence of the Holy Spirit on a daily basis?

_____
_____
_____
_____

3. In what ways might the Holy Spirit be inviting you toward sanctification? What needs to happen for you to accept that invitation?

_____
_____
_____
_____

> Heavenly Father, words cannot capture our gratitude for your infinite love and gentle grace. Through the work of your Son, we have been brought back to you…never to be lost again. Forgive us when we return to our old ways of sin and rebellion. Remind us of our true status: your beloved child. Guide us toward your Spirit's leading so that our will is a reflection of your will.
> Amen.

54   Friday

Romans 8:5-8 (ERV)

People who live following their sinful selves think only about what they want. But those who live following the Spirit are thinking about what the Spirit wants them to do.

Reflection

I've always loved the famous line out of the movie *Batman Begins*, "It's not who I am underneath, but what I do that defines me." In many ways that is true. Our actions lean toward reflecting our perceived self-identity. But for Christians, that is not the full truth. While our actions will always reflect some aspect of who we are, we cannot let that perspective rule the day. If we do, then we are in danger of remaining anchored in our old life.

If what we "do" is a definition of who we "are," we must concede that it is a sword that cuts in both directions. At times, it will reveal the stubbornness of residual sin, but at other times, it will unveil the goodness of God. The question then becomes who is wielding that sword?

As Christians, the Holy Spirit is always active in our lives. Whether we recognize it or not, the divine spark that resides within us is constantly moving, speaking, reassuring, convicting, and guiding. The invitation is to act in harmony and compliance with him, if for no other reason than it will lead to life and peace. But we can also ignore his offer by defying and disregarding his leading. We have the autonomy to pursue our own agenda.

However, whatever choice we make, the scandalous nature of Jesus' love and grace is the opposite of Batman's famous statement. It *is* who we are underneath, and *not* what we do that defines us. When we seek grace and accept the forgiveness of Christ, our identity is forever in him, no matter what we do.

Contemplation Questions

1. Is there a difference between how you see yourself and how God sees you? What does God see that you don't, or won't?

___

2. Do you detect the grace of Jesus as reconciling you toward God's view of you? Describe some of the ways that might be at work even now.

___

3. What steps could you take to lean more toward God's view of you? How will this change your perspective? How will it influence the way you live life?

___

> Jesus, we love you and seek your grace, even as we are stuck in our old patterns of living. We desperately need your Spirit to guide us away from our selfish and destructive patterns of living. Calm us and direct us to a posture of listening and learning. Lead us in your way of life and peace.
>
> Amen.

55 — Saturday

Father, Son, and Holy Spirit:

As we wind up this week, we are thinking back on how we navigated these last seven days–how we acted for good and how we caused harm; the times we were obedient and the times we rebelled. We are reminded that your love and grace has made us new, but we continually revert to our old ways.

Remind us of the reality of our lives. We have been brought back to you… never to be lost again. Let us recall our true status: your beloved child. Give us your peace and remind us that we are safe. Renew the invitation to participate with you in the cause of your kingdom. Guide us toward your Spirit's leading so that our will is a reflection of your will.

Grant us forgiveness and instill in us the strength to walk in the way you would have us go. Calm us and direct us to a posture of listening and learning. Lead us in your way of life and peace.

Amen.

Week 8

Zariquiegui, Spain

Week 9

It stands to reason, doesn't it, that if the alive-and-present God who raised Jesus from the dead moves into your life…
(MSG)

57 — Monday

Romans 8:9-11 (MSG)

It stands to reason, doesn't it, that if the alive-and-present God who raised Jesus from the dead moves into your life, he'll do the same thing in you that he did in Jesus, bringing you alive to himself? When God lives and breathes in you (and he does, as surely as he did in Jesus), you are delivered from that dead life. With his Spirit living in you, your body will be as alive as Christ's!

Reflection

Arguably, this is one of the most reassuring scripture passages in the entire *New Testament*. The Spirit lives within us, and better still, knows us intimately. It is comforting to realize that we are not alone, and we are not on our own. But what do we know about this ever-present companion in life?

The Greek word for spirit is *pneuma*, meaning wind, breath, air. It envisions a dynamic movement that cannot be visually seen. As words go, this is the perfect analogy for the Spirit. We only know there is wind or breath or air moving by seeing how it impacts what it touches, and the same is true for the Holy Spirit. We can't see the Spirit directly, but only by what he affects.

I intentionally use the personal pronoun of "he" for the Holy Spirit (although in the Greek, the word is gender neutral) because we cannot reduce him to a lifeless and nebulous kind of force or power. The Spirit is not an "it" because he has personhood and personality. Scripture tells us he is not oppressive or coercive, not a bully or a terrorist, nor does he torment us. Likewise, as a person, we have an invitation to develop a relationship, understanding him as our present-day Immanuel who speaks into our life in a way that no one else can.

Contemplation Questions

1. In what ways do you recognize the presence of the Holy Spirit in you?

___

2. What steps do you take to place yourself in a posture to receive the Spirit's guidance?

___

3. Do you recognize the invitations of the Spirit? If so, what might they be?

___

> Holy Spirit, how wonderful it is to recognize that we journey through this life together, and that with you we know God is always present. Forgive us when we ignore your voice or disregard your leading. Encourage us in assuming a better posture to hear you. Restore in us the joy of the relationship. As we embark on this week, lead us in the way we should go.
>
> Amen.

58

Tuesday

Romans 8:12-17 (MSG)

So don't you see that we don't owe this old do-it-yourself life one red cent. There's nothing in it for us, nothing at all. The best thing to do is give it a decent burial and get on with your new life. God's Spirit beckons. There are things to do and places to go!

Reflection

One of my favorite fictional movies is *Big Fish* (released in 2003). I like it because the main character, Edward, is given a vision early in his life that depicts exactly how he will die. We might think that is a dreadful event, but that is not how Edward received it. He saw it as a gift, and from that moment forward, he fearlessly faced all manner of trials and tribulations by reminding himself out loud: "This is *not* how I die." He lives with a brave and uncompromising outlook because he is no longer incapacitated by fear.

Back here in the real world, many people live with an approach opposite of Edward. They sense potential harm and possible death with every new encounter and circumstance. The guideposts for navigating through that kind of life are marked by fear and anxiety, subconsciously convinced that "this *might be* how I die." While the goal of this approach is to maximize longevity, it results in a sheltered life of hesitancy, timidity, and missed opportunities. It might produce a long life, but it will be short on engagement and fulfillment.

In this passage, Paul is reminding us to shake the shackles of fear and anxiety. In a roundabout way, he indicates that we will receive a vision far better than what the fictional Edward got. The reality of the promise we have from Jesus gives us an unshakeable source to be bold and courageous: "Whoever lives by believing in me will never die" (John 11:26). It gives us "an unbelievable inheritance." This endowment then empowers us to receive the guidance of the Holy Spirit free from the competing thoughts of worry and apprehension that hold us back. We are free to live the resurrection life.

Contemplation Questions

1. To what extent does fear shape the way you live your life?

_____

_____

_____

_____

2. How do those fears hold you back from living a fuller life in God?

_____

_____

_____

_____

3. If you had an absolute promise of safety, what might your life look like?

_____

_____

_____

_____

> Heavenly Father, what a gift you give us: life eternal–the reassuring reality that we have nothing to fear in death. Awaken us from our dread. Release us from our anxiety. Remind us that we are safely and permanently in your care. Invite us to re-enter our life and live it boldly for you and your kingdom.
>
> Amen.

59 — Wednesday

Romans 8:18-21 (MSG)

That's why I don't think there's any comparison between the present hard times and the coming good times. The created world itself can hardly wait for what's coming next. Everything in creation is being more or less held back. God reins it in until both creation and all the creatures are ready and can be released at the same moment into the glorious times ahead. Meanwhile, the joyful anticipation deepens.

Reflection

I get excited when planning for an outdoor adventure. I have always been drawn to exploring God's creation. To me, it is nothing short of a luxury to encounter God in the setting of his created world. I especially gravitate toward places that are natural, rugged, and pristine, free of humanity's unrelenting desire for smooth paths and square corners. The best part of these trips is not only what I've planned for, but the pleasant surprises that invariably arise once underway. Sights and experiences I never imagined introduce themselves like unexpected and undeserved gifts.

For example, every time I encounter the grandeur of the Rocky Mountains, I am awestruck. But the surprise is learning how much erosion and decay played into producing the beauty—because they are nothing more than remnants of something larger. They are like once mighty sandcastles that have been ravaged by the incoming tide. But the splendor is still present.

Creation functions the same in representing God's magnificence. While we see the present landscape and are mesmerized by its beauty, it is only revealing hints to something much more majestic. It is only an appetizer for what yet lays ahead. In the same way, it reminds us perhaps we would do better to see our life as an opportunity of time and space, not only to prepare for that adventure, but to fully appreciate what we will encounter once it is revealed.

Contemplation Questions

1. Do you have eager expectations that you are looking forward to? What are they?

   _____
   _____
   _____
   _____

2. What pleasant surprises has God revealed to you as you journey in life?

   _____
   _____
   _____
   _____

3. Can you discern how God is upholding and sustaining you in the journey?

   _____
   _____
   _____
   _____

Heavenly Father, we wait with great anticipation for when the skies roll back and the fullness of your kingdom is revealed. In the meantime, thank you for your Creation. We ask for patience and endurance for our current journey, and encouragement to continually search for the hints and indications of your amazing glory. Reveal yourself so that we may encounter delight and joy.

Amen.

60   Thursday

Romans 8:22-25 (NIV)

We know that the whole creation has been groaning as in the pains of childbirth right up to the present time. Not only so, but we ourselves, who have the firstfruits of the Spirit, groan inwardly as we wait eagerly for our adoption to sonship, the redemption of our bodies. For in this hope we were saved. But hope that is seen is no hope at all. Who hopes for what they already have? But if we hope for what we do not yet have, we wait for it patiently.

Reflection

Creation, what we call the "world," is a mixture of both beautiful and harsh environments. Some are the right mixture of sun, sky, and water, producing a lush and inviting backdrop that supports all manner of life. Others are stark and barren, revealing an unforgiving landscape where only the hardiest survive.

But we have also learned that Creation is always changing. Evidence has revealed that where ice once stood, temperate forests now stand. Where there once was jungle, only desert sand can be found. But it is exactly out of these inevitable and sometimes cataclysmic environmental transitions where the most astounding beauty is discovered.

As such, Creation is not only a reflection of God, but also an appropriate metaphor for the journey through life. It is a mixture of beautiful and harsh, a combination of blessings and adversity, a time of continual change and movement from one setting into the next. To be sure, these changes are sometimes unwelcomed, and frequently painful. But we also need to be open to the prospect that this is where the beauty of God is revealed in amazing and unexpected ways.

Contemplation Questions

1. Looking back on your life journey, how have blessings and adversity shaped who you are?

_____

_____

_____

_____

2. In those times when you are experiencing painful changes, where might God be at work in sculpting you?

_____

_____

_____

_____

3. Do you trust God is leading you toward your "best days"?

_____

_____

_____

_____

> Lord God, your Creation reflects how you are always on the move. You do not sit idle nor do you wallow in nostalgia. God, as you move, remind us of the ever-present invitation to join you in that movement. Forgive us in our stubbornness and extend to us patience from our complaining. Encourage us with the vision that our best days are yet ahead.
>
> Amen.

61 Friday

Romans 8:26-30 (MSG)

God knew what he was doing from the very beginning. He decided from the outset to shape the lives of those who love him along the same lines as the life of his Son.

Reflection

It is a core principle of Christianity that God is the supreme ruler of all of his Creation, including over humanity. However, Christians have different perspectives on who "makes the first move" in the relationship between humanity and God that leads to salvation. Indeed, this issue is probably the foremost distinction among the faith traditions.

Some believe that humans make the first move toward God by first accepting him into our hearts. That it is a choice that is ours alone to make, and if we so desire, can defeat the desires of the Creator of the universe with a simple "no." Others, such as myself, believe that it is always God–through the Holy Spirit–who makes the first move in salvation. In short, if God desires to save someone, that person will be saved, since it is only God who wields the power of salvation.

The fact that we are chosen by God for salvation should not evoke a reaction of smugness or pride, but rather, an attitude of gratitude. Nor should it make us doubt God's intention because of who he does or does not choose…not that we can ever be certain of it anyway. Rather, it is a mindset that recognizes the true scope of God's majesty and sovereignty, while at the same time, recognizing his benevolence and adherence to his promises by giving us the Holy Spirit.

Contemplation Questions

1. How is God completing what he started in you?

_____

_____

_____

_____

2. Do you recognize the ways that you minimize or deflect it away?

_____

_____

_____

_____

3. Where can you see the invitation of God's love in your present circumstance?

_____

_____

_____

_____

> Lord, we have only the smallest glimpse of your immense splendor and power. Yet, we strive to define you in ways that reduce you to a position of helplessness. Forgive our arrogance that we foolishly believe that we possess leverage against your mighty will. Remind us that we stand naked and defenseless before your glory–unable to utter a word. Yet, we do know–and completely rely upon–the perfect love expressed in your son Jesus who speaks grace to you on our behalf. Lord, we lay our lives before you. Your will be done.
>
> Amen.

62 — Saturday

Powerful Father, precious Son, and productive Spirit:

We praise you. We look to your Creation, and in it, see how you are always on the move. But you do not move alone. Instead, you invite us into the journey with you. Through the blessings of the ever-present Holy Spirit, we know that you are with us because you are *in* us.

Spirit, forgive us when we ignore your voice or disregard your leading. Forgive us for our stubbornness and our complaining. Forgive us when we stupidly believe we can resist your will. Forgive us when we refuse to recognize that in the end, we are hopeless and helpless without you.

Thank you, Jesus. You are the Messiah, the King, and the Ruler over all. Praise for your grace, your love, and your patience.

Restore in us the joy of the relationship that we have neglected and disrespected. Release us from our anxiety. Remind us that we are safely and permanently in your care. Invite us to re-enter our life and live it boldly for you and your kingdom.

Lord, we lay our lives before you. Your will be done.

Amen.

Saint-Jean-Pied-de-Port, France

Week 10

So, what do you think?
(MSG)

64 — Monday

Romans 8:31-39 (MSG)

So, what do you think? With God on our side like this, how can we lose? If God didn't hesitate to put everything on the line for us, embracing our condition and exposing himself to the worst by sending his own Son, is there anything else he wouldn't gladly and freely do for us?

Reflection

"With God on our side like this, how can we lose?" We should stop and reflect on that statement from verse thirty-one for a long while. How often do we lose sight of that simple truth? How much have we drained the vivid color and devastating detail from God's power of grace?

The closing of chapter eight sets forth the most powerful image of what Jesus does for us. He is our advocate, our lawyer in the heavenly court of God. But when we sin, we should never imagine that Jesus stands before God pleading a case of compassion on our behalf, as if he is begging the Father to give us "one more chance." To the contrary, the more accurate visual is to see Jesus calmly demanding the full application of the law.

This shouldn't surprise us. Remember, that in our sins, we have violated God's law. But also remember that in the fullness of God's law, the punishment for those sins was already satisfied by Jesus. Therefore, as a matter of law (and not compassion) we are set free. The penalty of sin and the sentence of death have no claim on us. Verse thirty-nine gives us the clearest and simplest statement of this reality: nothing will separate us from the love and grace of God. Not now. Not ever.

Contemplation Questions

1. Can you identify a particular fear, worry, or doubt that keeps you from the fullness of life God desires for you?

_____

_____

_____

_____

2. Are you able to detect and locate where God is present in the fear, doubt, or worry? If so, does he feel close or far away?

_____

_____

_____

_____

3. What would be God's part and what would be your part to experience release from that fear, worry, or doubt? Write it out and pray for it.

_____

_____

_____

_____

> Lord Jesus, you have set us free, so we are free indeed. Excuse us when we ignore the impact of that pardon on worries, anxiety, and doubt. Forgive us when we treat that gift with contempt and derision, acting as if we earned grace, or worse, are entitled to it. Lord, let us return to you in humility and repentance, and grab ahold of the fullness of life you have provided. As we start into this week, guide us in the way that we should go.
>
> Amen.

65

Tuesday

Romans 9:1-9 (MSG)

Don't suppose for a moment, though, that God's Word has malfunctioned in some way or other. The problem goes back a long way. From the outset, not all Israelites of the flesh were Israelites of the spirit. It wasn't Abraham's sperm that gave identity here, but God's *promise*.

Reflection

The modern proverb, "Blood is thicker than water," expresses the gravitational pull of the family bond. It is characterized by an unwavering loyalty and devotion that supersedes all other competing obligations. In the extreme, the relationship is revered above all else, and responsibilities toward serving it are venerated. Violating its norms and values are frequently punished through shame, isolation, and banishment.

Paul certainly experienced it toward the Jewish culture and religion in which he was raised. Breaking away from it clearly caused a deep pain that only comes with the grief of separation and the loneliness of exile. It highlights why it is so difficult for any of us to do it. Empathy and allegiance to "tribe" is something most of us can relate to, be it family, faith, or even our cherished sports team. We all want to belong to something bigger than ourselves that will provide us a sense of acceptance, security, and/or significance.

If there is "blood" that draws and holds us together, it is the blood of Jesus. It is not a bond based on heredity, ethnicity, culture, or class. Its clarion call is not enforced through humiliation, segregation, or threat of expulsion. To the contrary, it is one of invitation, gentleness, and love. More importantly, it is one that is given from above, not earned from below. We are not entitled to it, but are privileged to be included within it under its true name: the family of God.

Contemplation Questions

1. What does it mean to you to be part of a family? What expectations do you believe come with that connection?

   _____

   _____

   _____

   _____

2. Do you have confidence in the knowledge that you are a member of God's family?

   _____

   _____

   _____

   _____

3. And as a member of God's family, do you embrace your fellow family members no matter their heredity, ethnicity, culture, or class?

   _____

   _____

   _____

   _____

Heavenly Father, forgive us when we exclude and divide into factions of our own making; for all the times we assume the mantle of supreme authority instead of humble servant. Through your son, we are bonded to you in grace and love. On this day, may our lives reflect that distinctive difference. Give us peace in knowing we are a part of your family.

Amen.

66

Wednesday

Romans 9:10-18 (MSG)

Is that grounds for complaining that God is unfair? Not so fast, please. God told Moses, "I'm in charge of mercy. I'm in charge of compassion." Compassion doesn't originate in our bleeding hearts or moral sweat, but in God's mercy. The same point was made when God said to Pharaoh, "I picked you as a bit player in this drama of my salvation power." All we're saying is that God has the first word, initiating the action in which we play our part for better or worse.

Reflection

"That's not fair!" is the common cry of a disgruntled child. While fairness is typically confused with equal treatment (they are not the same), the motivation behind either remains consistent. It is an unyielding belief that we possess rights, even against God. To complain about fairness to God is to begin wrestling with the theological concept of his sovereignty. God is not afraid to grapple with us over these kinds of questions. Yet, we would be wise to be mindful of our biases and the subtle influences of our cultural norms regarding government, justice, and human rights.

For example, a single sentence in the preamble to the U.S. Declaration of Independence shapes our view on what we are entitled to as people: "We hold these truths to be self-evident, that all men are created equal, that they are endowed by their Creator with certain unalienable Rights, that among these are Life, Liberty and the pursuit of Happiness." While I am a huge supporter and beneficiary of the Declaration and all the laws, rules, and customs that have flowed from it, we need to be cautious against letting that perspective have an undue impact on our understanding of God. As theologians, we have to scrutinize any assertions made on behalf of our Creator, especially when it uses "self-evident" truths as a justification. We should question whether God has indeed relinquished his rights, and how that impacts our view of what Paul is telling us here.

As a starting point, can we at least admit that, in this present age, we are not familiar (let alone comfortable) with the concept of a king who has absolute power? Do we acknowledge that when God imposes his will upon the world, we don't get to vote on it, make an objection, or appeal to a higher power? Are we willing to concede that we stand naked and silent in front of God, possessing zero rights? In the end, God is sovereign. He holds all the cards. All we can rely upon is the promise of salvation and redemption given to us by his Son. The only right we have is the right of faith.

Contemplation Questions

1. How would you define "fairness"? And why is it so important?

2. Why are we desperate to believe that we possess inalienable rights?

3. What does it feel like to recognize that we can't demand fairness from God? What lessons can we take from this in our relationships with others?

> Heavenly Father, we humble ourselves in front of you. Forgive our hubris and arrogance. We come to you not with rights, but with prayers and supplications. Remind us of your awesome and indisputable power that always reflects your glory. May it strengthen our faith on this day.
>
> Amen.

67   Thursday

Romans 9:19-33 (MSG)

Are you going to object, "So how can God blame us for anything since he's in charge of everything? If the big decisions are already made, what say do we have in it?"

Who in the world do you think you are to second-guess God? Do you for one moment suppose any of us knows enough to call God into question? Clay doesn't talk back to the fingers that mold it, saying, "Why did you shape me like this?" Isn't it obvious that a potter has a perfect right to shape one lump of clay into a vase for holding flowers and another into a pot for cooking beans?

Reflection

If God chooses and rejects people without any regard to their character or autonomy, it raises the theological issue known as unconditional election. Typically, there are two objections against this line of reason. First, it would make God "unjust," and second, it wipes away personal responsibility in the salvation equation.

On the former, we can all agree that God is NOT unjust. However, we must also admit that we are wholly unprepared to assess what is "just" and what isn't. As noted yesterday, we are ill-equipped to raise a valid objection or call into question God's decisions. Simply put, humanity does not possess any rights before God.

As for the latter, Paul knew that exact objection would be raised, which is why he repeats it in verse 19: "One of you will say to me: 'Then why does God still blame us? For who is able to resist his will?'" (NIV). It is natural to assume we have personal responsibility in receiving salvation, because that is how we experience it. From where we stand, it is up to us, and us alone, to decide to give our lives to Jesus. But asserting that as a theology ignores what is told to us in scripture. Paul metaphorically points out that the clay doesn't tell the potter what to make. The purpose and shape of the vessel is entirely up to the potter.

Paul goes on to reassure us that the decision is not arbitrary. While God chooses and decides entirely based upon his own counsel, he does so to reveal his justice and power. Besides, grace is never given based on anything worthy we've done. It is a gift from God to us. If it is not given, we cannot receive it. If it is given, we cannot refuse it. In the end, God choosing who, when, and how salvation bestowed is indeed patently unfair. But then again, if it were truly fair, none of us would receive it.

Week 10

Contemplation Questions

1. Reflect on how you experienced receiving salvation from Jesus. Make a list of surrounding circumstances and factors that made that happen.

_____

_____

_____

_____

2. Review your list. Examine whether or not you had control over those circumstances and factors. Where do you detect God's presence in the midst of them?

_____

_____

_____

_____

3. Contemplate whether or not you would have received salvation in the absence of those circumstances and factors. How does that inform your perspective on God's power to choose who receives salvation?

_____

_____

_____

_____

> Heavenly Father, we humble ourselves in front of you. Forgive our arrogance. We come to you not with rights, but with prayers and supplications. Remind us of your awesome and indisputable power that always reflects your glory. May it strengthen our faith on this day.
>
> Amen.

68 Friday

Romans 10:1-3 (ERV)

Brothers and sisters, what I want most is for all the people of Israel to be saved. That is my prayer to God. I can say this about them: They really try hard to follow God, but they don't know the right way. They did not know the way that God makes people right with him. And they tried to make themselves right in their own way. So they did not accept God's way of making people right.

Reflection

Nobody walks around with the wrong theology. If we thought or believed it was wrong, we would change it. But change can be hard. Like tree roots, our long-standing beliefs and perspectives about God tend to grow more stubborn over time. We become complacent and see only what we want to see of God. If we're not careful, we begin to form him into an image of our own making, rather than searching for who he is.

That was certainly true of the covenant nation of Israel. God repeatedly tried to correct their increasingly wayward theology, but they were having none of it. They stuck to their rituals of the Temple, traditions of the Torah, and limited perspectives about who could, and couldn't, be included in the Kingdom. When God finally sent his one and only son, Jesus, they ignored the purest and truest theology of all time. They refused to change.

Does that make the pursuit of theology wrong? The answer is no. But it is helpful to remember that while God is perfectly immutable, our theologies regarding him are not. So, while God is unchanging, it doesn't mean he has stopped moving. He is on a continual quest to redeem and recall his people back to himself. From our end of the salvation equation, that presents as change, which can make us feel uncomfortable or obstinate. Perhaps it is helpful to remember that theology is not the task of "solving" God. On the contrary, it is the intentional and dedicated effort to engage with him in a meaningful way. We don't do it to confirm our preexisting suppositions. We do it to discover the magnificent mysteries of who he is.

Contemplation Questions

1. Have you ever changed any aspect of your theology about God?

   _____
   _____
   _____
   _____

2. What was the underlying cause for the change? How did you know it needed to change? How did the change impact your relationship with God? Did it draw you closer or push you further away from him?

   _____
   _____
   _____
   _____

3. Might God be inviting you even now to reexamine your theology? If so, how and why?

   _____
   _____
   _____
   _____

> Lord, forgive us for all the times we try to decipher and explain you and your ways, if only to ensure we're not found in violation. Eradicate our motivation of self-interest. Remind us to pursue you for the best and purest reason: love. As we wrap up our week, invite us into your presence so we may dwell in the peace and joy of who you are.
>
> Amen.

69   Saturday

Heavenly Father, Precious Son, Ever-Present Spirit:

As we enter into the end of the week, we take this time to set aside the things that have distracted and divided us. In its place we take on a posture of humility and an attitude of gratitude, remembering that through the sacrifice of Jesus, we have been set free, so we are free indeed.

We approach the throne and confess our sins over this last week.

    Forgive our mindset-filled constant worries, anxiety, and doubt.

    Forgive us our attitude of arrogance that results in behaviors of contempt and derision.

    Forgive us for all the times we try to decipher and resolve you and your ways, if only to ensure we're not found in violation.

    Forgive our motivation of self-interest.

    Forgive us when we exclude others and divide into factions of our own making.

    Forgive us for all the times we assume the mantle of supreme authority instead of humble servant.

Lord, let us return to you in humility and repentance. We ask that:

    You pour out your grace and love upon us.

    You remind us of your awesome and indisputable power that always reflects your glory.

    You invite us into your presence so we may dwell in the peace and joy of who you are.

    You lead us toward the fullness of life you have provided.

    Our lives reflect a distinctive difference that is found in you.

                                Amen.

Burguete-Auritz, Spain

Week 11

It's the word of faith that welcomes God to go to work and set things right for us.'
(MSG)

71   Monday

Romans 10:4-10 (MSG)

It's the word of faith that welcomes God to go to work and set things right for us. This is the core of our preaching. Say the welcoming word to God—"Jesus is my Master"—embracing, body and soul, God's work of doing in us what he did in raising Jesus from the dead. That's it. You're not "doing" anything; you're simply calling out to God, trusting him to do it for you. That's salvation.

Reflection

"Am I really saved?" It is not an uncommon question we ask ourselves from time to time. We wonder if salvation is as simple as it is stated in verse 9, "If you declare with your mouth, 'Jesus is Lord,' and believe in your heart that God raised him from the dead, you will be saved" (NIV). While the words are easy enough to say, the pivotal issue is the self-examination of our hearts.

There is a long-standing general rule in criminal law that prohibits a confession alone to be sufficient for a conviction in court. Rather, the confession must be supported by corroborating evidence that a crime did indeed occur. Without it, the confession is deemed untrustworthy and unreliable.

Perhaps this rule known as *corpus delicti* (Latin for "body of the crime") is a good metaphor for assessing what we believe in our hearts. Does the rest of the world see any proof that verifies our confession that Jesus is Lord? This kind of inquiry isn't a modern-day form of legalism, nor should we interpret it as works-based righteousness. To the contrary, it is an invitation and encouragement to be willing to back up our words with actions. It is nothing more than an act of trust that substantiates our faith.

Contemplation Questions

1. If a person is changed by Christ, what differences would we expect to see in that person? Think of some reasons why that is important.

   _____
   _____
   _____
   _____

2. Have you ever experienced a Christian behaving in an un-Christ like manner? How would you characterize the impact it had on the Gospel message of Jesus?

   _____
   _____
   _____
   _____

3. What proof of change does the world see in you? Consider writing them down.

   _____
   _____
   _____
   _____

> Lord Jesus, you love us unconditionally. You meet us where you find us, but you never leave us there. Reassure us in our doubts. Encourage us in our actions that reflect our trust in you. Send your Spirit upon us as we step into this new week.
>
> Amen.

72

Tuesday

Romans 10:11-13 (MSG)

Scripture reassures us, "No one who trusts God like this—heart and soul—will ever regret it." It's exactly the same no matter what a person's religious background may be: the same God for all of us, acting the same incredibly generous way to everyone who calls out for help. "Everyone who calls, 'Help, God!' gets help."

Reflection

We live in an era that is increasingly skeptical of anything that "sounds too good to be true." It is understandable given that we are constantly bombarded with free offers and amazing deals that really aren't when we get down to reading the fine print and disclaimers, or worse yet, when we become victims of an outright scam. It is understandable that we've grown. We've become wary of being taken advantage of.

As a result, it is no surprise that the response of many to the claim, "Everyone who calls on the name of the Lord will be saved," runs the gamut from disinterest to cynicism. It just seems too simple and easy. No one gets this kind of gift without some strings attached or preconditions to be fulfilled.

Yet, as hard as it may be for some to accept, it is that simple and easy. To be clear, the words given to us in scripture are not like a secret incantation that suddenly summons the genie from the magic lamp. God will not be fooled or manipulated into the salvation equation. But at the same time, the invitation to meet the Creator of the Universe doesn't require a speech or an elaborate religious ceremony. All it takes is the slightest and sincerest cracking of our heart toward God, and the Holy Spirit will rush in with grace, love, and power…and we will be forever changed. It is the most important help we will ever need.

Contemplation Questions

1. Recall moments or incidents when you opened your heart to God. How did it change or influence your life?

___

___

___

___

2. Have you experienced times when God "let you down" or "didn't deliver"? How did it change or influence your faith?

___

___

___

___

3. Ask God why salvation is so easy and subsequent faith is so hard. How does that change or influence your witness?

___

___

___

___

> Father in Heaven, forgive us for the lengths we will go to keep you at a distance. Remove from us the excuses and doubts that erode our trust and reduce our dependence on you. Lord, we recognize that you never force yourself upon us, but if we ask for your help–simple and direct–you will answer us. Thank you for that awesome privilege.
>
> Amen.

73 Wednesday

Romans 10:14-17 (NIV)

How, then, can they call on the one they have not believed in? And how can they believe in the one of whom they have not heard? And how can they hear without someone preaching to them? And how can anyone preach unless they are sent? As it is written: "How beautiful are the feet of those who bring good news!"

Reflection

It is paradoxical that in this day and age of instant communication that sharing the gospel of God with the people of the developed world still presents steep challenges. But it is not an issue of distribution or access. There are countless avenues to get the information about God in front of people. Rather, the problem revolves around authenticity and relevance. In short, is it real, and does it make a difference?

There is an old cliché attributed to St. Francis of Assisi, "Preach the gospel always, and only when absolutely necessary, use words." This missive highlights the need for our actions to speak louder than our words. This is gospel authenticity. Gospel authenticity recognizes the need for trustworthiness being part and parcel of any communication. Gospel authenticity is when our conduct is in alignment with our speech. Gospel authenticity is revealed in a humble and transformed life. But that only solves half the problem. The need for relevance remains.

What St. Francis actually wrote is far more nuanced and addressed this need for relevance. A better and more accurate translation of his words is, "It is no use walking anywhere to preach unless our walking is our preaching." Notice the movement required of the speaker: "walking to preach." He or she is on the move toward the listener, and not the expectation of it being the other way around. This is gospel relevance.

Gospel relevance happens when the bringer of the gospel meets those in need where they are, not where we think they should be. Gospel relevance occurs when there is a first-hand familiarity and compassion for the context and complexities of the listener. Gospel relevance values deeper connection over pontification.

Gospel authenticity and gospel relevance reflect the life pattern of Jesus, who never dwelled long in the places of power and prosperity. Instead, he was frequently on the move, an itinerant speaker to those who society had disregarded, abandoned, and deposited on the margin. This is why Romans 10:15 famously tells us, "How beautiful are the feet of those who bring good news!" (NIV).

Contemplation Questions

1. In what manner is "gospel authenticity" revealed in your life? How are you able to reflect God's truth and your faith to those you encounter?

_____

_____

_____

_____

2. On a scale of 1 to 10 (10 being highest), how would you rate your "gospel relevance"?

_____

_____

_____

_____

3. Using the number you assigned yourself above, what would need to happen to increase it by one?

_____

_____

_____

_____

> Lord Jesus, forgive us for our harboring and hoarding of your good news of salvation. Heal our wounds from rejection and ridicule from previous experiences. Coax us out of our immobility. Give us courage to once again move toward those who have yet to know your love and grace. May our actions and attitudes reflect the reality of who you are.
>
> Amen.

74 Thursday

Romans 10:18-21 (MSG)

But haven't there been plenty of opportunities for Israel to listen and understand what's going on? *Plenty,* I'd say.

> Preachers' voices have gone 'round the
>   world,
> Their message to earth's seven seas.

So the big question is, Why didn't Israel understand that she had no corner on this message?

Reflection

Paul borrows from Psalm 19 in the scripture for today. It begins this way:
> The heavens tell about the glory of God.
> The skies announce what his hands have made.
> Each new day tells more of the story,
> and each night reveals more and more about God's power.
> You cannot hear them say anything.
> They don't make any sound we can hear.
> But their message goes throughout the world.
> Their teaching reaches the ends of the earth. (NIV)

The words from both the Psalmist and Paul are the basis for the theological concept known as "general revelation." It asserts that God can be known to anyone who lives in this world because God is experienced through the marvel of nature. Not just the expanse of the world and all the life in it, but it's incredible intricacy and interdependency.

This should compel us to ask: "Where did all this come from?" Because when we look around us, we have to admit that the world is not self-explanatory. We are left with lingering questions: What was the source? How was it assembled? What or who holds it together? This is not to say that nature is a complete revelation of God, but rather, that it gives evidence there is a God.

Every day we are in the world, God, through his creation, gives us a reminder and extends an invitation. It is an encouragement to recognize that we have the privilege to be in a relationship with the one who created it all. It is an ongoing offer, so we are without excuse.

Contemplation Questions

1. Think about the place(s) where you feel most at one with God. How would you describe the experience?

   _____

   _____

   _____

   _____

2. Where might you be able to detect the beauty of creation in your everyday environment?

   _____

   _____

   _____

   _____

3. How might God be inviting you into his presence in the everyday environment? What needs to happen for you to accept this invitation?

   _____

   _____

   _____

   _____

> Father, you created the heavens and earth. Forgive us when we turn a blind eye to its beauty or grow complacent with its majesty. Remind us that each day we receive a visual reminder to draw closer to you. Let us rejoice in the privilege and flourish from the experience.
>
> Amen.

75   Friday

Romans 11:1-2 (MSG)

Does this mean, then, that God is so fed up with Israel that he'll have nothing more to do with them? Hardly. Remember that I, the one writing these things, am an Israelite, a descendant of Abraham out of the tribe of Benjamin. You can't get much more Semitic than that! So we're not talking about repudiation. God has been too long involved with Israel, has too much invested, to simply wash his hands of them.

Reflection

The nation of Israel clung desperately to its family of origin story. In their eyes, it defined who they were and what they could expect. Although they longed for a rescuer king, the Messiah, they refused to adjust their preconceived expectations. When Jesus did reveal himself, not only in person but in purpose, they looked away, their narrow hopes unsatisfied.

Unmet expectations can inflict harm in the conduct of our daily lives. We are forced to adjust and compensate. We must deal with our own disappointment and shattered anticipation. If we are unaware or unprepared, this can be especially dangerous when it comes to our faith in God. Our reactions range from confusion to despair. We feel ignored or even spurned.

For the Israelites, God didn't abandon them due to their rejection, but he didn't stop moving forward either. God's plan for his Kingdom and this world continues. The final events in the divine plan are relentlessly revealed with each new day.

But this does not mean we have a theology without love. God is never consumed with a laser-like focus such that he won't pause to dwell with us when we drag our feet. The Father is always available to us, no matter how stubborn we are in the moment. Should we display a willing desire, he will immediately enfold us back into the progress of his coming kingdom. That is an expectation we can hold onto.

Contemplation Questions

1. Have you ever felt ignored or abandoned by God? How did you experience it?

_____

_____

_____

_____

2. Make a list of expectations you have of God. Is it a long or short list? Are you able to point to scripture to support your expectations?

_____

_____

_____

_____

3. Examine whether you can reconcile your experience described in question 1 with your response to question 2.

_____

_____

_____

_____

> Heavenly Father, forgive our stubborn and unwarranted expectations. We fall into the trap of privilege, thinking our selfish desires supersede your perfect plan. Remind us of your sovereignty. Shower us with your love. Bestow your grace and invite us back into being part of the solution instead of the problem.
>
> Amen.

76   Saturday

Heavenly Father, Lord Jesus, and Holy Spirit:

We know that we are loved unconditionally. You meet us where you find us, but you never leave us there. Yet, we keep you at a distance. Your creation speaks to us every day, but we turn a blind eye to its beauty and grow complacent with its majesty. We continue to harbor our stubborn and unwarranted expectations thinking our selfish desires supersede your perfect plan.

Forgive us.

Remove from us the excuses and doubts that erode our trust and reduce our dependence on you. Mend our wounds that have kept us away. We recognize that you never force yourself upon us, but if we ask for your help–simple and direct–you will answer us.

Heal us.

Coax us out of our immobility. Give us inspiration to once again move toward those who have yet to know your love and grace. May our actions and attitudes reflect the reality of who you are.

Encourage us.

Send your Spirit upon us as we wind down this week.

                                        Amen.

Week 11

Iroz, Spain

Week 12

It's the same today.
(MSG)

78 Monday

Romans 11:3-6 (MSG)

It's the same today. There's a fiercely loyal minority still—not many, perhaps, but probably more than you think. They're holding on, not because of what they think they're going to get out of it, but because they're convinced of God's grace and purpose in choosing them. If they were only thinking of their own immediate self-interest, they would have left long ago.

Reflection

Over the course of history, the number of faithful followers of God has seemed to ebb and flow. There are times of ascendency and importance, followed by times of scarcity and irrelevance. Christendom has both ruled and has been relegated to exile. Rarely is its presence in culture steady, but thankfully, it is always persistent.

Here in America, Christianity is experiencing a significant downturn in both belief and participation. There is much hand wringing and angst during this current experience of being on the backside of the wave. Some try to explain it with finger-pointing and accusation, as if it were possible to hold back the tide with mere complaints. Far more lament and then simply abandon the bandwagon. But neither of those reactions are the way of a Christ-follower.

If we claim Christ, we do not wet our finger to determine which direction the prevailing wind is blowing. We understand that faith, and the discipleship that flows from it, is not a compulsory demand of God. As such, we don't wallow in nostalgia, nor do we seek the affirmation of popularity. Our task is simple: either we pick up our cross, or we don't.

But this much the Bible makes clear: even in the dispiriting times where God's people have suffered banishment and been consigned to insignificance, there has always been a faithful remnant. They have a resilient identity that values intimacy with God above all else. They practice quiet discernment and seek authentic community. They pursue what God lays before them. They have no interest in prominence or prosperity, but rather, only to share the true treasures of grace, love, redemption, worship, and service. That is what it means to be a disciple of Jesus, and it is enough.

Contemplation Questions

1. What draws you toward the practices of faith?

   _____

   _____

   _____

   _____

2. Do you find yourself thinking nostalgically about Christainity's place in culture?

   _____

   _____

   _____

   _____

3. In today's Christian environment, where do you stand? Do you point fingers or accuse? Have you cut and run? Or do you count yourself among the faithful remnant?

   _____

   _____

   _____

   _____

Lord Jesus, our battle against evil waxes and wanes, but your victory is never in doubt. Forgive us for the times when we are anxious or apathetic in our faith. May we grab onto the certainty of who you are and what you will do. Restore our confidence. Encourage us to be among the faithful remnant. Grant us your love and grace. Guide us as we start into this new week.

Amen.

79   Tuesday

Romans 11:7-10 (MSG)

And then what happened? Well, when Israel tried to be right with God on her own, pursuing her own self-interest, she didn't succeed. The chosen ones of God were those who let God pursue his interest in them, and as a result received his stamp of legitimacy. The "self-interest Israel" became thick-skinned toward God.

Reflection

When evil receives its just punishment, the righteous celebrate. This sentiment is frequently expressed in the Psalms. It fulfills our need that the world has been brought into balance, if only for a moment. It is a glimpse of "the way things ought to be" which much of humanity longs for. But what is the source of that longing? From where does it originate?

The context for Paul's quoting scripture is from Deuteronomy 29, where Moses is addressing the nation of Israel at the conclusion of 40 years in the wilderness. We should note that the cause of the people's blurred vision and impaired hearing was God himself. In the same way this happened to Pharaoh, it raises the contentious issue of God's sovereignty versus our free will. But this also exposes the nature of humanity. (For more, see previous entry #65 on Romans 9:10-18.)

We need to be reminded that humanity's short-sightedness and egocentric deafness are self-inflicted wounds. Wisdom and insight about God are spiritual gifts given by God, not part of our inherited DNA. If God leaves us to our unredeemed state, who are we to complain? If we bully our way through life, leaving a wake of destruction behind us, why should we be surprised? Just as it is in the natural world, the strong survive, the weak perish, and life moves on without remorse.

But if we seek something better, if we long for something different than what the world is currently serving up, then let us never forget that the perception of righteousness and justice originate from God, just as peace and reconciliation are gifts of the Spirit. Pursue one without the other and the only result will be frustration.

Contemplation Questions

1. What is it about the way of the world that causes you to grieve?

_____

_____

_____

_____

2. Where do you find hope in the face of your grief?

_____

_____

_____

_____

3. Where might God be inviting you to participate in his acts of justice?

_____

_____

_____

_____

> Heavenly Father, we humble ourselves in front of you. Remind us that we are blind and deaf without your presence in our life. Forgive our vanity and arrogance. Remind us of your awesome love, your powerful grace, and your unbendable will. May we detect within us the beautiful image of you. Strengthen our faith this day.
>
> Amen.

80   Wednesday

Romans 11:11-12 (MSG)

The next question is, "Are they down for the count? Are they out of this for good?" and the answer is a clear-cut *No*. Ironically when they walked out, they left the door open and the outsiders walked in. But the next thing you know, the Jews were starting to wonder if perhaps they had walked out on a good thing. Now, if their leaving triggered this worldwide coming of non-Jewish outsiders to God's kingdom, just imagine the effect of their coming back! What a homecoming!

Reflection

In some ways, the scripture for today reflects the wisdom found in the parable of the Prodigal Son told by Jesus in Luke 15. Although it is not a direct one-to-one correlation, it captures the stubbornness of the human heart to adhere to our own ways until the bitter end, only to discover it is not God's way.

Paul's declaration on the future of Israel should be instructive to us all. In short, he states that when it comes to love, grace, salvation, and redemption through God, it is never too late. We should never give up hope for those who have refused the invitation or stop praying for those who have turned away. God never abandons people, and neither should we.

But it is also worth noting that Paul doesn't make a declarative statement on the future of Israel. The Holy Spirit did not privilege him with that information. All he received is the encouragement of possibility, which is also instructive to us. We hope and pray for outcomes in people turning toward or returning to God, but with the recognition that those outcomes are strictly within God's purview.

Contemplation Questions

1. Have you in the past, or in the present, prayed for someone to come to faith?

   ___

   ___

   ___

   ___

2. Describe any outcomes you have detected from your prayers, including the impact it had on you.

   ___

   ___

   ___

   ___

3. Can you identify places of stubbornness that remain within your own heart and mind? How is God inviting you to pay attention to them?

   ___

   ___

   ___

   ___

> Lord Jesus, forgive us for our prodigal ways. We go astray and rebel. We are wasteful and excessive. We are brash and insolent. And through it all, you patiently wait for us to recover our senses and return to you. We are humbled by your forbearance. Infuse us with your love and compassion and instill in us a better sense of our true identity: your beloved child.
>
> Amen.

81 Thursday

Romans 11:13-15 (ERV)

Now I am speaking to you people who are not Jews. I am an apostle to the non-Jewish people. So while I have that work, I will do the best I can. I hope I can make my own people jealous. That way, maybe I can help some of them to be saved.

Reflection

Insiders vs. outsiders; haves vs. have nots; liberals vs. conservatives; jocks vs. nerds; gay vs. straight; black vs. white. These are but a few examples of the countless dichotomies that humans have created throughout time to separate people into opposing groups. It seems to be our compulsive default reaction.

The ancient Jewish culture certainly wasn't exempt from falling into this dynamic. Indeed, they were vastly more insular than the surrounding cultures, to the degree that it became a point of pride. It was a safe haven that provided them security, identity, and affirmation. However, as Paul points out, over-reliance on that strength turned it into a weakness. They were so protective of their theology and traditions that they missed the Messiah.

The same might be true for us if our theology and traditions become excessively inward-looking and narrow. A solid theology is a necessary companion for a strong faith, but if it results in categorizing people into groups of "the enlightened few" versus "the ignorant masses," we too have missed the Messiah. Our outlooks and traditions should never allow for the denigration and belittling of others.

Jesus gave the disciples, and us, one commandment to guide us in all matters of life and faith: "Love one another. As I have loved you, so you must love one another" (John 13:34). This indicates that any theology or traditions that lack love are worthless ones. It means we are right being love, instead of love being right.

Contemplation Questions

1. Using the list from the first paragraph of today's reflection, what categories would you place yourself in? What other categories would you use?

_____

_____

_____

_____

2. Do those categories capture the fullness of who you are? Why or why not?

_____

_____

_____

_____

3. How would you characterize your relationship with other people who are in different categories? In those instances, how can you become more loving without having to be right?

_____

_____

_____

_____

> Father God, forgive us for the division we create amongst ourselves, your beloved children. You invite us into a strong faith, but always require that it is lived out in love, grace, and service. Let us practice patience and peace with whoever you place in our path. Let our love be the beacon for drawing others to yourself.
>
> Amen.

82 Friday

Romans 11:16-20 (ERV)

It is as if some of the branches from an olive tree have been broken off, and the branch of a wild olive tree has been joined to that first tree. If you are not a Jew, you are the same as that wild branch, and you now share the strength and life of the first tree. But don't act as if you are better than those branches that were broken off. You have no reason to be proud of yourself, because you don't give life to the root. The root gives life to you.

Reflection

"By their fruit you will recognize them" is the famous statement given in Matthew 7. In the original context, it was a warning against false prophets. As a metaphor focuses on how our invisible inner spiritual life will be made visible to everyone else as witnessed by our thoughts, words, and actions. Good fruit will come from a healthy and vibrant spiritual life, and bad fruit from an unhealthy or non-existent spiritual life.

Paul uses the same metaphor, but with a different twist. The emphasis isn't so much on the kind of fruit that is produced (although that is important), but rather the source of any fruit production. If a fruit branch is deeply and correctly connected to the trunk, it will bear good fruit. If not, no fruit is forthcoming, and we are simply firewood.

This highlights how we frequently distort our relationship with God. We erroneously view the relationship as us producing good fruit independently, and then bring it to the Lord as a gift offering. That is akin to Old Testament sacramental thinking. A more accurate view is that the Lord is the one who produced the good fruit through us (and sometimes in spite of us). We get the credit, but he deserves the glory. Without his presence, we are nothing.

Contemplation Questions

1. Is it important to you to produce "good fruit" as part of your faith journey? Why or why not? If it is, make a list of that "good fruit."

___

2. As you consider your list, can you ascribe the source of each incident or example of bearing fruit? How much of it is of your own doing and how do you attribute it to God?

___

3. Can you detect the connection between the productivity of fruit and the healthiness of your relationship with Jesus?

___

> Lord Jesus, let your goodness and righteousness flow through us. Give us access to good words that reflect your truth. Inspire us to good deeds that reveal your love. Lead us to produce good fruit that is to the world's benefit and your glory.
>
> Amen.

83 — Saturday

Heavenly Father, Lord Jesus, and Holy Spirit:

We humble ourselves in front of you. Forgive our:

– anxious or apathetic faith

– vanity and arrogance

– rebellion and wandering away

– wasteful and excessive desires

– brash and insolent attitudes

– divisive behaviors.

Remind us that we are blind and deaf without your presence in our life. Your awesome love, powerful grace, and unbendable power will never lead us astray. You invite us into a strong faith, but require that it is lived out in love, grace, and service.

May we grab onto the certainty of you–who you are and what you will do. Restore our confidence. Remind us that the beautiful image of you lives within us. Encourage us to be among the faithful remnant.

Grant us your love and grace.

Let your goodness and righteousness flow through us.

Give us access to good words that reflect your truth.

Inspire us to good deeds that reveal your love.

Lead us to produce good fruit that is to the world's benefit and your glory.

Amen.

Week 12

Villatuerta, Spain

Week 13

If God didn't think twice about taking pruning shears to the natural branches…
(MSG)

85

Monday

Romans 11:21-24 (MSG)

If God didn't think twice about taking pruning shears to the natural branches, why would he hesitate over you? He wouldn't give it a second thought. Make sure you stay alert to these qualities of gentle kindness and ruthless severity that exist side by side in God—ruthless with the deadwood, gentle with the grafted shoot. But don't presume on this gentleness. The moment you become deadwood, it's game over.

Reflection

What is God the Father like? To answer that question, Paul paints a picture of God as an arborist or orchard farmer. The use of this simile makes the description of the Lord more emphatic and vivid for us, the reader, but it also highlights the limitation of any answer about God's character. In the search for understanding, we must be careful as we attempt to describe him only by his attributes and characteristics that are familiar to us.

That is not to say God is unknowable. There are, of course, aspects regarding him that we can know or experience. It includes things such as love, grace, mercy, patience, peace, goodness, holiness, truthfulness, humility, and faithfulness. They reflect the traces of God's hand in creating us so we can recognize how we are made in his image. There also is a side to God we can never understand. He possesses qualities that are unique to him that we will never share. It involves characteristics such as self-existence, infinity, unity, perfection, immutability, all-powerful, and all-knowing. As this part of his image will never be found in us, we must accept and submit to those attributes because they are beyond our comprehension.

In the end, we must concede that God is beyond "knowing" in any complete sense of the word. There is mystery to who he is. Yet, God is the one who seeks a relationship with his people. The Bible is, if nothing else, a compilation of narratives that reflect this. He wants to be known, and the best way for that to occur is for us to know his son Jesus. If we know the Son, we will know the Father.

Week 13

Contemplation Questions

1. Is it important for you to know as much about God as possible?

_____

_____

_____

_____

2. Contemplate how your efforts to know God better have influenced your faithfulness.

_____

_____

_____

_____

3. How is your faith impacted when encountering the mystery of God? (In other words, when God cannot be explained.) Has it ever damaged your relationship with him? How did you resolve it?

_____

_____

_____

_____

> Lord Jesus, we want to know you. Reveal yourself to us in your Word and by the actions of the Holy Spirit. Forgive us when our efforts lag. Encourage us in our attempts. Affirm us in our experiences. Guide us closer to you as we step into this new week.
>
> Amen.

86

Tuesday

Romans 11:25-29 (MSG)

From your point of view as you hear and embrace the good news of the Message, it looks like the Jews are God's enemies. But looked at from the long-range perspective of God's overall purpose, they remain God's oldest friends. God's gifts and God's call are under full warranty—never canceled, never rescinded.

Reflection

For most of us, there is no animosity towards Jewish people. Unfortunately, that has not always been the case in the history of the relationship between the Jewish and Christian faiths. It can be described as everything from isolation and ignorance to antagonism and violence. Recent iterations include the "Jewish Question" being raised in the mid-19th century and reaching its lowest point with the "Final Solution" by the Nazi's in the 1940s. As a whole, it has been a sordid record.

Into this bitter saga comes the verse of Romans 11:28: "for the sake of the Gospel, they are your enemies" (NIV) which, if read in isolation, certainly doesn't help the ill-informed biblical reader. If we are to ever rise above misunderstandings and bad theology, especially regarding Israel's place in the biblical narrative, we need a healthy understanding of the framework that organizes the bible. The theology of covenant provides this.

The bible is a book full of covenants. Indeed, the word covenant is incorporated into the two main sections of the bible, the Old and New "Testament." The word testament in Latin is the same word for covenant. Upon opening the book, we encounter a steady stream of examples of how covenants given in the former are fulfilled in the latter by the work and life of Jesus. Covenants are what bind those two volumes into one book.

The scope of covenant theology is a vastly deeper topic than we can unpack here. But it is helpful to understand that when we encounter a "covenant," it is critical to distinguish it from a "promise" or "contract." Although those terms are frequently interchanged, a covenant has an important distinction. It demands a much higher degree of compliance. While we might wiggle out of a promise, or be excused from the terms of a contract, covenants demand fulfillment regardless of whether or not the other party is doing his or her part. This applies to the situation of God's covenant with Israel. Although the Israelites turned away from the relationship, God hasn't–he will fulfill his covenant with them. And the same is true for us. God's covenant with us through Jesus will never be canceled or rescinded.

Contemplation Questions

1. Reflect on your posture toward people of the Jewish faith. Describe what you think and feel toward God's covenant people.

   _____

   _____

   _____

   _____

2. Do you detect any evidence of prejudice or superiority in your posture? Describe what that looks like. Were you aware of them, or is it surprising?

   _____

   _____

   _____

   _____

3. How might Jesus be inviting you forward into adjusting your posture that better reflects the attributes of God?

   _____

   _____

   _____

   _____

Heavenly Father, forgive us of any prejudices, and erase them from our identity. We seek you, but may it never be at the expense of anyone else. Lord, in the mystery of your will, we surrender our suppositions. In the power of your love, we extend patience, understanding, and grace. Heal our many wounds. Restore us to where we need to be.

Amen.

87

Wednesday

Romans 11:30-32 (ERV)

All people have refused to obey God. And he has put them all together as people who don't obey him so that he can show mercy to everyone.

Reflection

As humans, we spend an awful lot of time and energy separating ourselves into smaller groups. They might be identified by ethnicity, nationality, religions, financial position, politics, and even sports teams. The dividing lines are a mosaic of different attributes, beliefs, aspirations, and affiliations—all in the effort to make ourselves distinctive from our fellow humans.

All this effort devoted to what separates us rather than what unites us ignores a very basic and simple fact: we all have rebelled against God, and we are all doomed by our sin. It is the single unifying fact that levels the playing field across the entire spectrum of humanity. None of us can look at anyone else and think ourselves higher, better, or even different, because all of the distinctions we strive so hard to attain make zero difference to God.

But there is another fact that unites us. We all share in the offer of mercy by God. He doesn't play favorites. He harbors no prejudices or biases. He does not discriminate based on our self-identity. He is not swayed by our distinctions. His love and grace are equally accessible to all.

Perhaps, if we truly recognized our shared predicament as well as the equal opportunity of rescue, we would display more patience and place more trust in one another. We would see the benefit of harmony and set aside our discord. Maybe it starts with us taking small, but intentional, steps that acknowledge the reality that we share more in common than what makes us different.

Contemplation Questions

1. What "smaller groups" of culture do you belong to or identify with?

    _____

    _____

    _____

    _____

2. Examine how your self-identity in those groups can mesh or clash with your identity as a Christian. Is it surprising or confirming?

    _____

    _____

    _____

    _____

3. Do you detect an invitation to change because of it? Describe why.

    _____

    _____

    _____

    _____

> Lord Jesus, forgive our striving for superiority or for elevating ourselves over others. Instill within us the reality of our situation–that we all are broken and in need of a savior. Give us patience and humility in our interactions. Heal our many wounds. Restore us to where we need to be.
>
> Amen.

88 Thursday

Romans 11:33-36 (MSG)

Is there anyone around who can explain God?
Anyone smart enough to tell him what to do?
Anyone who has done him such a huge favor
   that God has to ask his advice?
Everything comes from him;
Everything happens through him;
Everything ends up in him.
Always glory! Always praise!
   Yes. Yes. Yes.

Reflection

These closing verses of chapter 11 are called a "doxology." This Greek word has two components to it: doxa meaning 'glory' and logia meaning 'saying.' It is a saying of praise of God. There are a number of recognized doxologies found in both the Old and New Testament, all characterized by expressions of acclaim and wonder about God.

Why is it important?

If we are going to pursue theology, we must also possess a doxology. If we seek to acquire deeper knowledge about God, but it doesn't cause a sense of awe and wonderment, then we've missed an essential attribute of theology. It means our approach to theology is flawed, and we missed its primary purpose. Discovering more about God should always lead to praise.

Contemplation Questions

1. Where in life and faith do you encounter God with wonderment and glory?

___

2. How do you connect what you know about God (theology) to your sense of awe *in* God (doxology)?

___

3. How would someone else experience and describe the way you worship God?

___

> Heavenly Father, we stand in awe of the depth of the riches of the wisdom and knowledge of who you are. Forgive us for forgetting that your judgments are unsearchable, and your pathways are untraceable. All things known and unknown, seen and unseen, come from you and belong to you. To you, God, be the glory forever and ever.
>
> Amen.

89 Friday

Romans 12:1-2 (MSG)

So here's what I want you to do, God helping you: Take your everyday, ordinary life—your sleeping, eating, going-to-work, and walking-around life—and place it before God as an offering.

Reflection

One of the better-known statements within Romans is, "Offer your bodies as a living sacrifice" (NIV). In writing this, Paul cleverly flips the Old Testament religious regulations regarding sacrifice to reveal a stark difference on how we are to live with Christ in our lives.

Under the old system, the rituals for temple sacrifices are spelled out in detail in the Book of Leviticus. It specifies what kind of animal can be used, how it is to be sacrificed, and what sin it absolves. Whatever animal is used, the rules are consistent in demanding that it is free from any defects. The underlying value being communicated is that it isn't really a sacrifice if all that is being offered up are lame or useless animals.

In contrast, we are encouraged to offer our bodies, which for most of us, are far from perfect. But that is exactly the point. God accepts us where he finds us. He doesn't demand flawlessness, but he does desire faithfulness. Faithfulness is best expressed in our actions and behaviors. In other words, what we do *while in our bodies*. It doesn't operate to resolve our sin (Jesus already did that), but it does lead to transformation. That, in turn, leads to alignment with God's will.

Contemplation Questions

1. Write down a description of your body.

_____
_____
_____
_____

2. Did you use physical terms? Intellectual descriptions? Spiritual?

_____
_____
_____
_____

3. How would these three different descriptors combine to describe offering your body to God as an act of worship?

_____
_____
_____
_____

> Heavenly Father, we come to you with all of our flaws, mistakes, and failures. We ask for forgiveness. Restore us with renewed courage and confidence. Guide us as we end this week. Let our bodies and our lives be conducted as a praise offering to you.
>
> Amen.

90   Saturday

Heavenly Father, Lord Jesus, and Holy Spirit:

We come to you with all of our flaws, mistakes, and failures seeking forgiveness. We continually strive for our own superiority at the expense of others. We repeatedly refuse to acknowledge your sovereignty and glory in fear of dimming our own need for validation. But as we acknowledge that your judgments are unsearchable, and your pathways are untraceable, we surrender our indefensible position. You are God and we are not.

As we stand in awe of the depth of the riches of the wisdom and knowledge of who you are, we ask for your presence. Reveal yourself to us in your Word and by the actions of the Holy Spirit. Let the power of your love heal our many wounds. Let the understanding of your nature give us patience, understanding, and grace.

Encourage our attempts and affirm us in our experiences. Guide us closer to you, and to you may be all glory forever and ever.

                                      Amen.

Week 13

Cirauqui, Spain

Week 14

In this way we are like the various parts of a human body.
(MSG)

92 Monday

Romans 12:3-5 (MSG)

In this way we are like the various parts of a human body. Each part gets its meaning from the body as a whole, not the other way around. The body we're talking about is Christ's body of chosen people. Each of us finds our meaning and function as a part of his body.

Reflection

We live life through the lens of the individual self. Our thoughts, words, actions, and deeds are driven largely by our needs and our own best interest. There are times when we bow to the needs and interests of other individuals and groups, such as our families, employers, and communities, because of our allegiances and obligations. But, by and large, we see ourselves–and our physical bodies–as independent and self-contained beings.

Paul challenges our perspective of individuality–at least as far as it impacts our life in Christ, which of course, is everything. We are not our own and we are not on our own. We belong to Jesus as part of his body. Paul expands on this analogy in his first letter to the Corinthians (Chapter 12), and both there and here, he highlights the absurdity of forgetting how interconnected we are with one another through Christ.

To take a slightly different tack from Paul, imagine if I were to strike you with my hand and then say defensively, "It wasn't me, it was my hand." You would find that ridiculous. The same applies to when we view ourselves as faithful believers but still divided and separated. The lowest common denominator is not us as individuals. It is us as the church.

This is why Paul starts with the admonition of not thinking more highly of ourselves than we ought. Genuine humility is the building block for shared unity. It is the realization that we are all in this together. Of course, this won't suddenly produce a conflict-free church. But at the very least, it will encourage us to collectively turn our attention to our Savior, and we (and the world we live in) will be better for it.

Contemplation Questions

1. Identify the situations where you subjugate your interests for that of a group or community of people. In what ways is that affirming? In what ways is it challenging?

___

2. Do you consider yourself generally to be a humble person? Are there areas in your life where humility is a problem?

___

3. How do you differentiate between a positive self-esteem and humility? Where is God in the midst of that difference?

___

> Lord Jesus, forgive us our selfish ways when we seek what is best individually instead of what is best for your kingdom. Remind us that we have unity in you and in you alone. Give us humility. Give us patience. Give us the strength and courage to set aside our own agenda and pursue your will and your way.
> Amen.

93   Tuesday

Romans 12:6-8 (MSG)

If you preach, just preach God's Message, nothing else; if you help, just help, don't take over; if you teach, stick to your teaching; if you give encouraging guidance, be careful that you don't get bossy; if you're put in charge, don't manipulate; if you're called to give aid to people in distress, keep your eyes open and be quick to respond; if you work with the disadvantaged, don't let yourself get irritated with them or depressed by them. Keep a smile on your face.

Reflection

This is one of those instances where Eugene Peterson's paraphrase is absolutely spot on. He captures the essence of what Paul is communicating about the relationship between spiritual gifts and the grace that it extends. Let me explain.

Verse 6, using a literal word-for-word translation of the Greek, starts this way: "Having the charisma in the charis." In the dictionary of biblical Greek, these two words are sequentially located next to each other. *Charis* means "grace" and *charisma* is translated as "gifts." This is more than a play on words, although we should tip our hat to Paul's creative phrasing that makes it memorable (at least to readers fluent in Greek). It perfectly expresses the truth that God's grace IS a gift, but far more than that, it is a gift that keeps on giving.

God has created each of us uniquely with special abilities that serve the kingdom and each other. That is expressed as our "gifts." But it is God's grace, through the work and sacrifice of his son Jesus, that reveals and launches those gifts. Just like they appear in the dictionary, they come to us sequentially. In other words, *charis* inspires *charisma*. But it doesn't stop there.

God's gift of *charis* keeps multiplying, diversifying, and advancing through time and history as long as we are faithful in our own given *charisma*. To repeat the well-worn phrase, we keep "paying the gift forward." So the next time we are prompted by the Holy Spirit to make use of our special charisma, recall the *charis* that started it all.

Contemplation Questions

1. God's grace inspires our gifts. What *charisma* is revealed through the *charis* in your life?

   _____

   _____

   _____

   _____

2. How do you pay grace forward?

   _____

   _____

   _____

   _____

3. Read again what Peterson transcribes: "Don't take over. Don't get bossy. Don't manipulate. Be quick to respond to people in distress. Don't get irritated or depressed with the disadvantaged." Do any of these sound like you? If so, what new steps can you take to change that behavior?

   _____

   _____

   _____

   _____

Father in heaven, honor and glory to your name. You have done far more than rescue us from sin and death. You have called us into your service. You have given us the privilege to be the announcers of your *charis* through our special charisma. Sharpen and refine us in that gifting. Encourage and guide us in its use. May we never neglect it or take it for granted.

Amen.

94 Wednesday

Romans 12:9-10 (ERV)

Your love must be real. Hate what is evil. Do only what is good. Love each other in a way that makes you feel close like brothers and sisters. And give each other more honor than you give yourself.

Reflection

The English word "love" is a positive one. It is a term that conveys warmth and affection. But it is also used in extremely broad ways. We carelessly bandy it around in our daily conversation, using it to express a spectrum of feelings. It covers everything from our emotional attachment to our spouse and children to describing how we feel about our favorite pair of jeans. We've turned "love" into such a flexible word that it has lost its shape and meaning.

Yet for all the varied ways we use the word, it remains the best descriptor of what lies at the very core of God's character. It is the central value of his agency on earth and in heaven as revealed in his son Jesus and activated through the Holy Spirit. It is the single commandment we were given to live by—making it the lifeblood of our faith.

Without love, nothing else matters. We either stop using the word, or we start living it out authentically. The scripture for today gives us simple guidance on where to begin: depart from evil. Cling to what is good. Honor others above ourselves. Do these, and scripture promises our life will thrive.

Contemplation Questions

1. How would you define "love" to someone who is new to the English language?

2. How is the fullness of God's love for you received and experienced in your life?

3. What does love ask of you toward others?

> Holy Spirit, forgive us for the ways we have distorted the meaning of love. We practice selfishness instead of sharing. We pursue gain instead of generosity. We promote hate instead of healing. Invite us back into your presence and let us rediscover the true value and significance of your love. Restore our vision and let us practice what you have taught to us to our benefit and your glory.
>
> Amen.

95 Thursday

Romans 12:11-13 (NIV)

Never be lacking in zeal, but keep your spiritual fervor, serving the Lord. Be joyful in hope, patient in affliction, faithful in prayer. Share with the Lord's people who are in need. Practice hospitality.

Reflection

The bestselling book *Faster: The Acceleration of Just About Everything* summarized various studies showing the pace of life has increased dramatically in the modern age. Moreover, rather than improving life, it is directly associated with detrimental health effects. In the years since it was published (1999), the dynamics impacting pace have increased many-fold.

But we already knew this intuitively. Despite an onslaught of technology that allows us to communicate quicker, complete tasks faster, and become more efficient, we feel like there is less time available. Even though our span of years is increasing, the quality of it is decreasing. The progression of our individualistic and production-focused culture has eroded any sense of personal time or space. At some point, we need to examine if this is leading us toward the fullness of who God created us to be.

The response to this increasing pressure is not to give up and lie flat in protest. Rather, it is to take a more measured approach. Paul gives us simple instructions for navigating the days of our lives. He is reminding us that faith is a journey, not a race. It requires more stamina than speed. His approach is neither hurried nor complicated: be diligent and not lethargic. Be fervent, not apathetic. Rejoice with hope and patience in tribulation. Most of all, be constant in prayer regardless of the situation.

Contemplation Questions

1. How would you describe the pace of your everyday life? Is it hurried and fast or slow and lethargic?

___

2. How do your faith practices correlate to the pace of your life? Are they hurried and fast? Measured and slow?

___

3. Imagine where and how you might encounter God if you were to change the pace of your life. What do you see?

___

> Heavenly Father, forgive us as we willingly speed through our days. Although we recognize the need to slow down, we're unwilling to address our addiction to constant stimulation. Invite us back to the healthy place of dwelling with you and serving in your kingdom. Restore to us the proper balance of task and time.
>
> Amen.

96   Friday

Romans 12:14-16 (ERV)

Wish only good for those who treat you badly. Ask God to bless them, not curse them. When others are happy, you should be happy with them. And when others are sad, you should be sad too. Live together in peace with each other. Don't be proud, but be willing to be friends with people who are not important to others. Don't think of yourself as smarter than everyone else.

Reflection

We do not hand out the title of "enemy" to just anyone. Our enemies earn that moniker. Our feelings toward them are never neutral. To the contrary, we experience a visceral reaction that looks for revenge. Not only do we want to hurt them back in equal strength, but we also want to pile on additional punitive punishment. So when we read that we should "Bless those who persecute you; bless and do not curse them," we struggle mightily to comply. It is easy to say but much more difficult to obey. On its face, the directive does not provide resolution to our pain or comfort in our loss–let alone our sense of justice or fair play.

But there is something worse than our pain or the injustice we feel that results from hating our enemies. Not only does it knock the foundation out from under the gospel message, but it also destroys us along the way. It is a trap that feeds into our own hidden insecurities of faith. It impoverishes us in the experience of God's grace. It exposes our lack of trust in what Jesus did for us and reveals our disbelief in the redemption of all things in the end.

Hating our enemies is not really about enemies at all. It is about us and God. It is a reflection on our relationship with the One who gave it all to save us. Because if we hate, we have excluded the possibility of love. And without love, nothing else in faith works.

Contemplation Questions

1. Make a list of your enemies. Make a notation on whether or not they know you personally, and if they are aware of your feelings toward them.

___

2. Next to each person on the list, describe the hurt or pain that you have experienced because of them. Do you notice an internal desire to hurt them in return?

___

3. What can you do between yourself and God to release your feelings? Is there something you can do with the person you hate?

___

> Jesus, forgive us for our hate. Although we recognize the need to love, we're unwilling to let go of our animosity toward others. Heal us from our hatred. Invite us back into the fold of your love, and let it inspire us to share it with everyone, especially with those who intend us ill will.
>
> Amen.

97 — Saturday

Heavenly Father, Lord Jesus, and Holy Spirit:

Honor and glory to your name. Not only have you rescued us from sin and death, you invite us to participate with you in your kingdom work. You give us the privilege to be the announcers of your *charis* through our special charisma.

We ask forgiveness for our selfish ways. We speed through our days, unwilling to address our addiction to constant stimulation. We are hoarding instead of sharing. We hate instead of love. We do what is best for us instead of what is best for your kingdom.

We ask for healing and restoration. Remind us of everything we find in you: unity instead of division, humility instead of arrogance, patience instead of aggravation. Invite us back into your presence and let us rediscover the true value and significance of your love. Give us the strength and courage to set aside our own agenda and pursue your will and your way.

Amen.

Week 14

Mañeru, Spain

Week 15

Don't hit back; discover beauty in everyone.
(MSG)

99 Monday

Romans 12:17-19 (MSG)

Don't hit back; discover beauty in everyone. If you've got it in you, get along with everybody. Don't insist on getting even; that's not for you to do. "I'll do the judging," says God. "I'll take care of it."

Reflection

These three verses contain wisdom on how to deal with people who don't share our perspective on living life. The second verse says, "If it is possible, as far as it depends on you, live at peace with everyone" (NIV). How does one possibly do that authentically within our current culture? With the rise and celebration of individualism, the sense of security from collective values and mores has faded. With the advent of the internet and social media, we are subjected to an avalanche of differing opinions, perspectives, and convictions. Taken together, we are constantly being stretched and challenged in our own positions.

Sometimes it feels as if we are at war, and it is all we can do to defend our thoughts and beliefs. If we are convinced that we hold the high ground of truth, the typical response is to become defensive and argumentative, sometimes militantly so. If we treat truth as relative, we offer no resistance, and simply escape the conflict by going along to get along. Neither approach is biblical.

The 19th century preacher Charles Spurgeon repeatedly used a sermon illustration that likened defending the truth and wisdom of the bible to trying to defend a caged lion. It was wasted effort since it would be better to simply open the cage door and let the lion defend itself. We can draw a lesson from that illustration. When disagreements arise, we can start with a simple self-examination exercise. We should ask ourselves, "Am I engaging in this to 'win' (to be right), or am I doing this to 'learn' (to gain understanding)?" This doesn't mean we concede the truth, but rather, we stop trying to weaponize it for our own edification. Instead, we recognize that God is the final arbiter of truth. In contrast, our duty is to practice what Jesus offers us as truth: his grace, his humility, and his peace.

Contemplation Questions

1. If you engage in the use of television news or social media, what emotions do they stir up in you? Do you detect feeling defensive and argumentative?

   _____
   _____
   _____
   _____

2. Do you find that you try to defend God's truth? Describe what that looks like.

   _____
   _____
   _____
   _____

3. How willing are you to let God set everything right? If the gospel can defend itself, what might be your role?

   _____
   _____
   _____
   _____

> Heavenly Father, too often we are only interested in being right instead of being faithful. We want to win rather than wanting to serve. Forgive our false pride and weak witness. May we step aside to your leading and let your truth prevail. Give us patience. Grant us peace. Send your Spirit upon us, we pray.
>
> Amen.

100 — Tuesday

Romans 12:20-21 (NIV)

Do not be overcome by evil, but overcome evil with good.

Reflection

It is said that in the never-ending battle between good and evil, evil only prevails when good does nothing. In large part that is true, but there is a caveat to this pithy phrase. Until Jesus returns, evil will always exist, and it will count innumerable victories during that time.

Although we can never eradicate evil, we can frustrate its intent and blunt its impact. We do this when we don't contribute to the problem by unleashing additional malevolence as our response. The first step, then, is not repaying evil with more evil. Although we may think it will comfort us or bring about justice, that kind of action is the evil of revenge. As Christians, we shouldn't engage in revenge.

What to do then? God frequently invites us to respond in ways that are not natural to us. For example, in the face of ridicule and condemnation, we are encouraged to act with honor and grace. In the presence of malice, we are urged to offer kindness. We could continue with an endless list of contrasts between actions that are evil and responses that are good. The key is recognizing that few of them are instinctive. This means we must be attentive, prayerful, and obedient to the leading of the Spirit. Then we will be doing the hard work of overcoming evil with good.

Contemplation Questions

1. In your context (where you live, work, and play) are you aware of examples of evil at work? Describe it.

   _____
   _____
   _____
   _____

2. What instinctual responses do you notice that rise up inside of you when encountering the evil in your context? How do you react?

   _____
   _____
   _____
   _____

3. Do the words "honor," "grace," and "kindness" reflect your responses and reactions? If not, what ways can you incorporate them?

   _____
   _____
   _____
   _____

Lord Jesus, forgive our responses that contribute to evil's continued existence in the world. Restore our character, honor, and identity that comes through your grace. Teach us, through your Holy Spirit, how to react with good when tempted to do otherwise. Inspire us to sacrifice for your name and for your glory.

Amen.

101 — Wednesday

Romans 13:1-7 (MSG)

Be a good citizen. All governments are under God. Insofar as there is peace and order, it's God's order. So live responsibly as a citizen. If you're irresponsible to the state, then you're irresponsible with God, and God will hold you responsible. Duly constituted authorities are only a threat if you're trying to get by with something. Decent citizens should have nothing to fear.

Reflection

Obey the government. Submit to the authorities. Pay your taxes. Respect your leaders. These can be challenging words for Christians to apply to life no matter where we live in this world. But this is asking far more than refraining from grumbling about what the governing authorities are deciding and doing. It directs us to trust in God when those decisions and actions extract a significant cost or confront a deeply held conviction.

These words are not cheap talk from Paul. He writes this in the context of a Roman government that was decidedly not Christian. Indeed, at the time, the church was in its infancy, and the religion of Christianity was deemed an "illegal superstition" within *Pax Romana*. It was a crime that carried with it significant penalties. Yet, he says he trusted God because it was God who placed them in power in the first place.

Paul trusted God in his situation. Do we trust God in ours? In this age of heightened partisanship, Romans 13 should give us pause the next time we feel the urge to express our opinions on the current political/social/cultural situation. This does not mean that we don't give them voice, but we do so absent of inflammatory and derogatory rhetoric. Nor does it mean we stop working toward justice and peace, but we do so with civility and a measure of deference. It asks for a deeper trust in God despite whatever the earthly authorities might be deciding or doing in the moment.

Contemplation Questions

1. Where do your political and faith beliefs align? Where do they separate?

   _____
   _____
   _____
   _____

2. How do Paul's admonitions reflect on your approach to combining the two?

   _____
   _____
   _____
   _____

3. How do you view people whose political and faith beliefs do not align with yours? Would a casual observer be able to detect a Christ-like perspective?

   _____
   _____
   _____
   _____

Holy Spirit, forgive us for all the times when we rant and rage against those in authority over us. Remind us that you have power over the whole world, and nothing exists without your permission. Give us humility to see your plan. Give us patience to wait on your timing. Give us wisdom to see your power and presence. Give us opportunities to be your servants of justice and peace. Even so, come Lord Jesus.

Amen.

102 — Thursday

Romans 13:8-10 (ERV)

You should owe nothing to anyone, except that you will always owe love to each other. The person who loves others has done all that the law commands.

Reflection

The wisdom of these verses cannot be fully appreciated apart from what we read yesterday (Romans 13:1-7). Yesterday, we encountered what God says we owe to the government and society. Here, we are told what we owe to each other as fellow citizens: love.

As noted last week, the English word "love" is a term that encompasses a wide spectrum of feelings and actions. In today's scripture, Paul gives sturdy guideposts on how to live out that broad word "love" via a reference to the Ten Commandments. It is important to notice that it is an illustration, not a prescription. It is an "including but not limited to" kind of example.

This is important because any definition of love requires the flexibility to express it in a way that fits each unique situation. In other words, we cannot escape the need of acting with love with the excuse that it didn't fit a predetermined criterion. Indeed, Jesus left us with that same broad and adaptable commandment, "Love one another as I have loved you. By this the world will know you are my disciples" (NIV). We should then continually look at how Jesus responded to a similar situation and then pattern ourselves after him.

Contemplation Questions

1. If you were asked to define the word "love," what words and descriptions would you use?

_____

_____

_____

_____

2. Would your definition change when describing the love of Jesus?

_____

_____

_____

_____

3. How would it apply to us loving others in the same way Jesus loved us?

_____

_____

_____

_____

> Jesus, your love is so tall, wide, and deep. It is broad enough such that it covers the whole world, and yet it is specific enough that it embraces each of us. Forgive us for all the ways we have turned away, rejected, or ignored your love. Invite us back into the security and affirmation of your warm embrace. Remind us of who we are. Show us the fullness of who you created us to be. Give us the courage and aptitude to reflect and share that love to all we encounter, but especially to those who are in need.
>
> Amen.

103 — Friday

Romans 13:11-14 (ERV)

I say this because you know that we live in an important time. Yes, it is now time for you to wake up from your sleep. Our salvation is nearer now than when we first believed. The night is almost finished. The day is almost here. So we should stop doing whatever belongs to darkness. We should prepare ourselves to fight evil with the weapons that belong to the light.

Reflection

We live in a daily rhythm of days and nights. A repeating cycle of bright sunshine and the dim shade of darkness. For most of us, we are awake when it is light and use the nocturnal time to rest and sleep. We mark the passing time with the number of sunrises and sunsets. That may be our physical reality, but Paul tells us here that it is not our spiritual reality. From a spiritual perspective, we are living in a time of perpetual darkness. This is a discordant thought, so what are we to make of it?

One need not read long in the Bible to discover that darkness is used repeatedly as a metaphor. We encounter it in the opening words of Genesis. The world is described as a chaos of darkness into which God speaks light into existence. As beautiful as that is, we should note that the darkness did not disappear. From that point forward, it is continually used to describe all manner of hardships. It can represent evil and eternal punishment, refer to spiritual blindness, or express sorrow and grief. In short, it is an allegory for the multitude of challenges we face in life and faith.

But as we continue to read, we also discover that darkness does not win. It does not prevail because scripture repeatedly tells us that God freed us from its power through the sacrifice of his Son. We will be brought into his presence–the kingdom of light. As such, we are urged to put the darkness behind us and prepare for the coming of day. Much like getting up in the morning, we are encouraged to dress ourselves in the grace and love of Christ.

Contemplation Questions

1. Can you identify the factors or situations that cause you to sink into, or remain stuck in, darkness? Make a list of as many as you can think of.

___

___

___

___

2. Now consider experiences that have brought you into the light. Again, make a list of as many as you can think of.

___

___

___

___

3. In your responses to the above questions, when and where do you detect the presence of God?

___

___

___

___

> Lord Jesus, as we end another week, forgive us our sins and the acts of darkness we have inflicted on the world. Restore us as we turn toward the sunrise of your love. Revive us as we bask in the light of your grace. Give us the strength and encouragement to bring your presence into the places that need it most.
>
> Amen.

Saturday

Heavenly Father, Lord Jesus, and Holy Spirit:

Too often we are only interested in being right instead of being faithful. We want to win rather than wanting to serve. Our responses contribute to evil's continued existence in the world rather than overcoming it. We are guilty of false pride and weak witness when we rant and rage against those in authority over us.

Teach us through your Holy Spirit. Inspire us to sacrifice for your name and for your glory. Remind us that you have power over the whole world, and nothing exists without your permission. Give us humility to see your plan. Give us patience to wait on your timing. Give us wisdom to see your power and presence. Give us opportunities to be your servants of justice and peace.

Restore us as we turn toward the sunrise of your love. Revive us as we bask in the light of your grace. Remind us of who we are. Show us the fullness of who you created us to be. Give us the strength and encouragement to bring your presence into the places that need it most. Send your Spirit upon us, we pray.

Amen.

Week 15

Grañón, Spain

Week 16

Welcome with open arms fellow believers who don't see things the way you do.
(MSG)

106   Monday

Romans 14:1 (MSG)

Welcome with open arms fellow believers who don't see things the way you do. And don't jump all over them every time they do or say something you don't agree with—even when it seems that they are strong on opinions but weak in the faith department. Remember, they have their own history to deal with. Treat them gently.

Reflection

When Paul wrote this, there were a relatively small handful of Christ followers spread out within the Roman empire. But even then, there were differences between them—in what they believed and how they worshiped. It was to be expected from a budding faith movement. As such, he advocated for an approach that didn't "quarrel over disputable matters."

Fast forward two millennia and it is a completely different story. In today's world there are more than two billion people who identify as Christian. However, within that number we find an astounding diversity of beliefs, theologies, practices, and traditions. We only need to look at a local directory of churches to see that Christians also identify as Baptist, Catholic, Reformed, Lutheran, Methodist, and Pentecostal to name just a few, not to mention the multitude of non-denominational churches.

I often say that the "Church" (large C) is not a monolith, it is a mosaic. It is made up of thousands of different pieces, each reflecting Jesus in their own unique way. But I am just as guilty as anyone of trying to distinguish between which one is "right" and which one is "wrong." It usually boils down to whomever believes like me is right, and everyone else is wrong. It is because none of us believe we are walking around with the wrong theology.

So how do we reconcile our particular perspectives of the faith with everyone else's? That is the subject matter for all of Romans 14. But verse 1 of the chapter begins with a call for tolerance, especially over the "disputable matters." Tolerance doesn't require us to abandon our theology, but it does ask us to refrain from breaking fellowship. As Paul spent the whole of chapter 13 reminding us, we are the body of Christ. We are not our own, and we are not *on* our own. We belong to Christ, and by necessity, to each other.

Contemplation Questions

1. Are you able to articulate your theological beliefs? Are any of those beliefs negotiable or flexible? Why or why not?

___

2. How would you describe your tolerance toward theological beliefs that differ from yours?

___

3. What is your guess to the following question: "How many different denominations are there in the world?" (Non-denominational churches are not part of this number. So, for example, the Roman Catholic Church counts as one.) Google the question. What is your reaction to the number? What does that number say about God?

___

> Heavenly Father, forgive our arrogance and intolerance toward fellow believers in your Son Jesus. Remind us that our only comfort in life and in death is that each of us is not our own, but we belong, body and soul, to our faithful savior. Restore us in your patience. Equip us in your love. Engage us to reflect all of it to the world.
>
> Amen.

107 — Tuesday

Romans 14:2-4 (MSG)

For instance, a person who has been around for a while might well be convinced that he can eat anything on the table, while another, with a different background, might assume he should only be a vegetarian and eat accordingly. But since both are guests at Christ's table, wouldn't it be terribly rude if they fell to criticizing what the other ate or didn't eat? God, after all, invited them both to the table.

Reflection

The two major demographics in the early church were non-Jewish Gentiles and Jewish converts. (In fact, the early church was seen as a schism from the Jewish faith.) There was major friction over church culture and practices between them. This encompassed three major topics: food, circumcision, and holy days. Non-Jewish Christians were critical of continued observance of Jewish religious practices. Jewish Christians were reluctant to let them go because they were so integral to their original faith formation.

For us, it is unfathomable, if not ludicrous, to be fighting over a food preference as a matter of faith. Not to be irreverent, but it seems that a "meat lover vs. vegetarian" debate should be confined to pizza orders, not philosophical disputes. Yet, the power of scripture is not that it records contextual details of a long-ago argument, but that it reveals the persistent brokenness of the human heart. It forces us to recognize that our distrust and disparagement of anything we deem "different" is a dynamic that continues to this day. The topics may change, but human behavior does not.

Paul admonishes all of us to drop the matter as unimportant because it dilutes the simple truth that God accepts all who come to him with a genuine faith. Jesus is the crucial truth, not the food they ate long ago or the religious ritual we prefer today. We need to return our focus to what unites us more than what separates us.

Contemplation Questions

1. Do you have any religious rituals that are non-negotiable? How do those rituals contribute to a better understanding and practice of your faith?

___

2. Have you ever encountered faith practices that make no sense to you or that you reject? Can you describe the underlying reasons for your response?

___

3. What are the essential ingredients for a genuine faith in Jesus?

___

> Lord Jesus, forgive our divisive thoughts and ways. As much as we want to occupy your judgment seat, remind us that no one receives salvation except through you.
>
> Amen.

108 — Wednesday

Romans 14:5-9 (NIV)

For none of us lives for ourselves alone, and none of us dies for ourselves alone. If we live, we live for the Lord; and if we die, we die for the Lord. So, whether we live or die, we belong to the Lord. For this very reason, Christ died and returned to life so that he might be the Lord of both the dead and the living.

Reflection

Healthy religious traditions are important to our faith. They draw us closer to God and keep us tethered to our beliefs. They provide a sense of community and belonging. We pass down collective memory and meaning through them. However, traditions without understanding render them useless.

In Romans 14, Paul is urging us to dig into the "why" behind our faith traditions. If we don't understand the motivation for doing them and the underlying values they are trying to communicate, then they are nothing more than mindless incantations and mysterious rituals. Therefore, he tells us that we should focus on knowing–and practicing–our own traditions rather than wasting time and energy on critiquing the traditions of others.

The last three verses of our scripture remind us (yet again) of the simple truth that, as Christians, we don't live just for ourselves. We live for the Lord. So, we let our lives, our faith, and our traditions reflect that purpose. Likewise, it says our dying is also for the Lord, and in either case of living or dying, we belong to the Lord. More importantly, this is the exact reason Jesus died and rose again. He is the Lord over life and death and everything in between, including all our beliefs and traditions.

Contemplation Questions

1. Identify any traditions (faith-based or not) that you observe or practice in your life. Why are they important to you? What does it contribute to your sense of well-being or self?

___

2. What faith-based rituals or traditions add meaning to your faith? How are they a reflection of Jesus?

___

3. Which faith traditions are you critical or dismissive of? Where do you detect God in your attitude?

___

> Holy Spirit, we repent from throwing stones at other religious practices while willfully neglecting our own. We ask you to forgive our hardened hearts toward unfamiliar traditions when they are faithfully and earnestly pursuing a relationship with the Father, the Son, and with you. Grant us your grace. Restore us in your patience. Equip us in your love. Engage us to reflect all of it to the world.
>
> Amen.

109 — Thursday

Romans 14:10-12 (MSG)

So where does that leave you when you criticize a brother? And where does that leave you when you condescend to a sister? I'd say it leaves you looking pretty silly—or worse. Eventually, we're all going to end up kneeling side by side in the place of judgment, facing God. Your critical and condescending ways aren't going to improve your position there one bit.

Reflection

Before I became a Christian at age 37, a large part of my resistance to faith was seeing how Christians treated other Christians. For instance, how Protestants spoke about Catholics, or how non-denominational churches viewed those from established denominations. From my perspective, it made no sense that they all worshiped the same God, and yet easily fell into "despising" and "passing judgment" on one another. If this was their witness of the Gospel, it had the opposite effect on me.

Verse 10 gives us a stern warning: "Why do you judge your brother or sister? Or why do you treat them with contempt?" (NIV) Notice that the directive is pointed toward a reactionary attitude that does not reflect Christ. It is not discouraging us from discernment, nor does it mean abdicating our theology and religious practices. Those are the very things that draw us closer to God. Rather, Paul is pointing out that it is neither healthy for our faith nor helpful for our theology when we focus on why everyone else is mistaken in their view of God.

The bottom line is that we will answer to Jesus for our time on earth–no one else. That means none of us has the privilege of the judgment seat for the simple fact that it belongs solely to Christ. Therefore, we must speak with deference and react with humility. Just like Jesus, we need to err on the side of grace.

Contemplation Questions

1. Do you notice within you a critical attitude toward other Christian faith traditions? Describe both what you object to and the way you experience it.

2. Can you describe what is at stake in your attitude or perspective? In other words, why is it important to you?

3. What is the role of God's grace in the midst of your reactions, criticisms, and perspectives?

Lord Jesus, forgive us for always trying to occupy the seat that only belongs to you. It is you, and you alone, who will judge. Remind us that the only thing we will be privileged to do with your seat is bow down before it. Even so, we humbly ask: grant us your grace. Restore us in your patience. Equip us in your love. Engage us to reflect all of it to the world.

Amen.

110 — Friday

Romans 14:13-14 (NIV)

Therefore let us stop passing judgment on one another. Instead, make up your mind not to put any stumbling block or obstacle in the way of a brother or sister.

Reflection

Human walking is frequently described as "controlled falling." In the movement of walking, the lead foot stretches out, plants itself on the surface, and stabilizes our weight. This allows the trailing leg to leave the ground, swing forward, and duplicate the process. Without conscious thought, we are able to propel ourselves where we need to go. But if anything interrupts this repeating cycle, it is no longer "controlled falling," but just plain old falling. None of us welcome the experience of tripping and falling. It causes everything from embarrassment to pain and injury. This is why the scriptural warning against anyone being a "stumbling block" resonates with us.

The term "stumbling block" is an idiom that traces its origin back to a litany of laws given in Leviticus 19. The literal commandment is against placing something in the path of a blind person that would cause them to trip, but euphemistically means, don't lay a trap that would cause someone to sin. (It is also where we get the word "scandal" from the Greek word *skandalon*.) Being a "stumbling block" implies that it is an inadvertent rather than an intentional act. Thus, the admonition is a call to awareness. It is thinking and acting in ways that considers how it impacts the spiritual obedience of others. It seeks to avoid unintended consequences because if it is premeditated or deliberate, that is called by another name: evil.

As brothers and sisters in Christ, and being part of Christ's body, we have an obligation to one another's health and well-being. This is especially true for our spirituality. The injuries and consequences of sin are far worse than the physical. So we pay attention to what could lead others away from God. In short, practicing self-awareness and self-denial, if called for, is fulfilling the commandment to love one another as we love ourselves.

Contemplation Questions

1. How do you practice self-awareness? How might you become more self-aware?

2. Have you ever witnessed behaviors in others that you thought would lead them away from God? Are you aware of your own behaviors that could potentially lead others away from God?

3. What would you sacrifice or deny yourself to assist someone else's faith?

> Lord Jesus, forgive us if we have contributed to someone going astray. Remind us that we are not on our own. We belong to you, and we belong to each other. Lead us in ways we can encourage and strengthen each other for our benefit and for your glory. Guide us into your presence as we end this new week.
>
> Amen.

111 — Saturday

Heavenly Father, Lord Jesus, and Holy Spirit:

We ask for your grace and seek your forgiveness for our continuing arrogance and intolerance. We are guilty of tearing down the religious practices of others while willfully neglecting our own. We are more interested in trying to occupy the seat that only belongs to you.

Remind us that our only comfort in life and in death is that each of us is not our own, but we belong, body and soul, to you, our faithful savior. It is you, and you alone, who will judge. Remind us that the only thing we will be privileged to do with your seat is bow down before it. Lead us in ways we can encourage and strengthen each other for our benefit and for your glory.

Grant us your grace. Restore us in your patience. Equip us in your love. Use us to reflect your love to the world.

Amen.

Week 16

Burgos, Spain

Week 17

God's kingdom isn't a matter of what you put in your stomach...
(MSG)

113 Monday

Romans 14:15-18 (MSG)

God's kingdom isn't a matter of what you put in your stomach, for goodness' sake. It's what God does with your life as he sets it right, puts it together, and completes it with joy. Your task is to single-mindedly serve Christ. Do that and you'll kill two birds with one stone: pleasing the God above you and proving your worth to the people around you.

Reflection

There is a remarkable incident that is described in both the Gospel of Mark and Luke. The disciples witnessed someone driving out demons in the name of Jesus. But instead of celebrating the event, they try to stop the man. Later they complain to Jesus about the incident and justify their actions on the rationale that "he does not belong to our group."

Sadly, this type of reaction is all too common among Christians—especially at the church level. We are competitive against one another. Like children that long for validation, we want to prove that we are the exclusive favorite of the Father. It has a tendency toward hoarding God's glory to our own particular manner of doing or viewing things, rather than delighting in the diverse ways God's grace expresses itself. We are more invested in comparing rather than rejoicing.

Speaking against this flawed approach, Jesus' reply to the disciples is instructive. He says, "Whoever is not against us is with us." Recall those words the next time we feel the pangs of jealousy about the success of another church. Remember the value being communicated when we start to elevate ourselves at the expense of another ministry. The whole effort and focus of faith is found in the name by which we identify ourselves: we are Christians. We are all about Christ, not about us. Anything that lifts his name and promotes his glory is a victory for us all.

Contemplation Questions

1. Do you detect jealousy in yourself over the "success" of another Christian, ministry, or church? What are the details of the situation that fuel your feelings?

_____

_____

_____

_____

2. Can you identify a need within you that is going unfulfilled through what you are feeling? What is it? Is it a healthy need or a selfish one?

_____

_____

_____

_____

3. Using your imagination, if God gave you the same level/manner of success, how would your faith and your life be different? Would your inner need be fulfilled? How else might God meet that need?

_____

_____

_____

_____

> Lord Jesus, forgive us when we tear others down in the vain hope to build up our flagging faith. We repent of our destructive ways of comparing and criticizing while ignoring the work of your kingdom. Remind us that our true identity is found only in you. Reassure us that we are all favored by your love and grace. Restore us to the kingdom tasks you have placed in front of us. Lead us in the way we should go.
>
> Amen.

114

Tuesday

Romans 14:19-21 (ERV)

So let's try as hard as we can to do what will bring peace. Let's do whatever will help each other grow stronger in faith. Don't let the eating of food destroy the work of God. All food is right to eat, but it is wrong for anyone to eat something that hurts the faith of another person. It is better not to eat meat or drink wine or do anything else that hurts the faith of your brother or sister.

Reflection

An edifice is defined as a large and imposing building, but size alone does not characterize it. Massive warehouses or sprawling housing units, while sizable, do not fall under that rubric. On the other hand, an edifice does require functionality; otherwise, it wouldn't qualify as a building. Thus, an edifice is both practical and inspiring, designed to both serve and instruct.

When we encounter an edifice, and experience a positive reaction, we are *edified*. This word is a descriptor that we encounter frequently in the Bible. Literally, it means to "build up." The NIV translates Paul's statement in Romans 14:19 this way, "Let us therefore make every effort to do what leads to peace and to mutual edification." The ESV states it slightly differently, "So then let us pursue what makes for peace and for mutual upbuilding."

In short, Paul tells us that we have the power to accomplish that in each other. We can edify one another by promoting one another's growth in our discipleship. We accomplish this by using the building blocks of wisdom, piety, obedience, and holiness. Remember, scripture teaches us that each of us is a "temple" of the Holy Spirit. (A temple is an excellent example of an edifice.) This means we can both receive and provide the building blocks of service and instruction from and to each other.

Contemplation Questions

1. Can you recall an example of a building or structure that evokes a feeling of encouragement, awe, or peace within you? What about it caused those emotions?

   _____

   _____

   _____

   _____

2. In the same vein as the question above, identify a person that "built you up."

   _____

   _____

   _____

   _____

3. How might God be calling you to serve as his agent of building up someone else?

   _____

   _____

   _____

   _____

> Father in Heaven, holy and wonderful is your name. You are the source of all wisdom and righteousness. You build us up by your love and grace, and you give us salvation through your Son. We are edified in your presence. May we turn toward people and provide encouragement and strengthening to everyone we encounter this day.
>
> Amen.

115 Wednesday

Romans 14:22-23 (MSG)

Cultivate your own relationship with God, but don't impose it on others. You're fortunate if your behavior and your belief are coherent. But if you're not sure, if you notice that you are acting in ways inconsistent with what you believe—some days trying to impose your opinions on others, other days just trying to please them—then you know that you're out of line. If the way you live isn't consistent with what you believe, then it's wrong.

Reflection

Recent research estimates that there are 2.5 billion people who identify as Christian. The vast majority belong to over 44,000 different denominations (not counting non-denominational churches). To give some perspective, the Catholic church accounts for more than half of the total number of believers. On the other hand, membership in a denomination that has 250,000 members would only represent .0001% of the total number. I like to joke that it is a wonder how all the other believers got it wrong.

Even within Protestantism alone, there are an incredible number of different beliefs and practices. Like the early Christians of Paul's time, we can be critical, and even hostile, toward fellow believers over these differences. Paul cautions us not to be. Instead, he says, "So whatever you believe about these things keep between yourself and God." (NIV)

It is a difficult thing in our own faith journey to believe a certain way when so many other Christians believe differently. Our beliefs strengthen and comfort us in times of trial. Our theology fortifies and edifies in times of searching, but ultimately, our faith is a matter between us and God. We will answer to him for what we believe and pursue. Whatever that might be, we need to recognize that it needs to be done in a spirit of love and grace.

Contemplation Questions

1. What theological beliefs that Christians differ over are critical to your faith? Can you identify why are they critical to your faith?

   _____
   _____
   _____
   _____

2. Do you find it difficult to love someone who has different Christian beliefs than your own? How would you describe what you are feeling if it is not love?

   _____
   _____
   _____
   _____

3. How might you follow Paul's instruction to "keep it between yourself and God"? What steps could you take towards expressing love for believers whose theology doesn't align with your own?

   _____
   _____
   _____
   _____

> Lord Jesus, forgive our judgmental ways. In seeking you, we are so apt to point out the wrongs of others, if only to avoid facing our own sins. Remind us that our chief priority is our personal relationship with you. Lead us in ways that we can discover our own beliefs that don't come at the expense of others. Guide us into your presence for our own benefit and for your glory.
>
> Amen.

Thursday

Romans 15:1-6 (MSG)

Those of us who are strong and able in the faith need to step in and lend a hand to those who falter, and not just do what is most convenient for us. Strength is for service, not status. Each one of us needs to look after the good of the people around us, asking ourselves, "How can I help?"

Reflection

We all want to stand on the mountaintop, but getting there is another story. Having spent a fair amount of time hiking in the Colorado Rockies, I've learned there is more to a successful hike than just having the right gear and sufficient provisions. It involves the intangible things that we carry inside of us instead of stuffed in a backpack. It is being equipped with the right mindset.

The first is endurance. Any activity at altitude requires different expectations from our bodies than we have at lower elevations. Because of the thin air, breathing becomes intentional instead of instinctive. The pace is more measured instead of spontaneous. One does not rush up a mountainside. Often, I would resort to the simple tactic of putting my head down and counting my footsteps toward a goal. Upon reaching it, I would look up to see where I was, and then decide if I could do more or needed to rest.

But just as important as endurance, if not more so, was encouragement. Expressions of affirmation and mutual support from hiking partners might contain words of hope about what lay ahead, or it might be reminders of how far we had come. Sometimes it was commiseration with what we were going through. Other times it was reassurance in our abilities. No matter what form the encouragement took, it invariably kept me from spinning on my heels and returning to the trailhead.

Paul tells us here that the scriptures are filled with stories of people who demonstrated endurance and encouragement but could do so because God was the underlying source of both. He explains that we can have what our Biblical heroes had: the Father's comfort and consolation. Jesus' stamina and perseverance. The Holy Spirit's understanding and awareness. It is equally accessible to us as it was to them, but only if we are willing to share it with each other. And if we do, we too can reach the mountaintop.

Contemplation Questions

1. Have you had times in your faith where sheer endurance was the only thing that kept you going? Can you recall the surrounding circumstance? What or who kept you going?

   _____
   _____
   _____
   _____

2. Conversely, have you ever gone through a "mountaintop experience" in your faith? Can you remember what led you to it? Was it hard or easy? Who else was present? How did they help you, or you them?

   _____
   _____
   _____
   _____

3. Where was God in the midst of either of the experiences in questions 1 and 2? How might God be inviting you to be an encouragement to another weary traveler?

   _____
   _____
   _____
   _____

> Heavenly Father, come to us when we feel defeated. Rescue us when we feel trapped. Bring us near when we feel lonely. Pour out your strength so we can respond with endurance. Send your peace and love so we can experience your encouragement. Guide us to the mountaintop so we can see your glory, and in turn, reflect it to all we encounter.
>
> Amen.

The Redeeming Road

117

Friday

Romans 15:7-13 (MSG)

So reach out and welcome one another to God's glory. Jesus did it; now *you* do it! Jesus, staying true to God's purposes, reached out in a special way to the Jewish insiders so that the old ancestral promises would come true for them. As a result, the non-Jewish outsiders have been able to experience mercy and to show appreciation to God. Just think of all the Scriptures that will come true in what we do!

Reflection

Insiders vs. outsiders has long been the dynamic problem in the Christian church. Typically, if we invite people to explore our faith, it follows these three steps: Step 1: Believe–like we do. Step 2: Behave–like we tell you to. Step 3: Belong–once you sufficiently look, think, and act like we do. We never find this discipleship pathway in the New Testament.

Jesus never vetted his disciples with a litmus test of beliefs before inviting them to follow him. Instead, he welcomed them into a faith journey that had the grace and sufficient margin to patiently absorb their objections and misconceptions. He loved first and taught second. And when the disciples failed, as they often did, Jesus didn't expel them from his company, but always looked for ways to redeem and restore. Remember, even Peter was welcomed back into the fold.

This approach was reinforced when Jesus left the disciples with the words of the Great Commission, which as Andy Stanley points out, doesn't say, "Therefore go and impose my teachings, values, and worldview on all nations, threatening them with judgment and destruction if they don't obey everything I have commanded you." To the contrary, Jesus commanded us to love one another as he loved us because he knows this is what will make "outsiders" become "insiders."

Contemplation Questions

1. Have you ever felt like an outsider? Are you able to recognize where you are in the position of an "insider"?

   _____
   _____
   _____
   _____

2. Can you think of ways that discrimination influences God's work in his kingdom here on earth?

   _____
   _____
   _____
   _____

3. What are the challenges to reaching out and embracing others who are different from you? How can you overcome them?

   _____
   _____
   _____
   _____

> Lord Jesus, forgive our tribal ways. Give us pardon for when we treat people as "other" when they don't look, think, act, or speak like we do. Lead us in your ways of grace and patience that they might see your presence and receive your love. Guide us as we end the work week.
>
> Amen.

Saturday

Father, Son, and Holy Spirit:

This week you have been pointing out our judgmental and tribal ways. We treat people as "other" when they don't look, think, act, or speak like we do. You have held up a mirror to our souls, and we now see how we eagerly tear others down in the vain hope of building up our flagging faith. How ready we are to point out the wrongs of others, if only to avoid facing our own sins.

We repent of our destructive ways of comparing and criticizing while ignoring the work of your kingdom, and ask for your forgiveness and pardon for our discriminatory ways. Remind us that our true identity is found only in you. You are the source of all wisdom and righteousness, and you pour out your love and grace.

Restore us to the kingdom tasks you have placed in front of us. Rescue us when we feel trapped. Bring us near when we feel lonely. Pour out your strength so we can respond with endurance. Send your peace and love so we can experience your encouragement. Remind us that our chief priority is our personal relationship with you, but that doesn't have to come at the expense of others. Guide us into your presence for our own benefit and for your glory.

Amen.

Week 17

Navarrete, Spain

Week 18

You seem to me to be well-motivated and well-instructed...
(MSG)

120 — Monday

Romans 15:14-16 (MSG)

You seem to me to be well-motivated and well-instructed, quite capable of guiding and advising one another. So, my dear friends, don't take my rather bold and blunt language as criticism. It's not criticism. I'm simply underlining how very much I need your help in carrying out this highly focused assignment God gave me, this priestly and gospel work of serving the spiritual needs of the non-Jewish outsiders so they can be presented as an acceptable offering to God, made whole and holy by God's Holy Spirit.

Reflection

Living Jesus, by Luke T. Johnson, was the first book I was assigned to read in seminary. While the subject matter of the book was obvious, that isn't what stuck with me. Rather, Johnson wrote something that sustained me through the rest of my seminary career, so much so that I took the time to rewrite it on the first page of every notebook I used during my time there. He said, "Learning demands suffering because it is painful to open the mind and the heart to new truth. Both for good and for bad, for loss and for gain, personal learning is always accompanied by suffering, and patience is the virtue that makes such suffering positive and meaningful. We endure for the sake of an education."

This quote is applicable far beyond seminary. It is appropriate for life because it is a never-ending learning experience. We are constantly encountering, processing, and absorbing new facts and knowledge. It is how we successfully navigate an ever-changing world. But it is just as applicable to our faith and our theology.

God is continually inviting our hearts and minds into new realities of how to love and live like his son Jesus. This was as true for Paul then as it is for us now. Sometimes what we learn is to our gain, but just as frequently, it is to our loss because of the sacrifice it involves. Yet, we continue our pursuit of Jesus for the sake of growing more like him. We endure so we can know him better.

Contemplation Questions

1. Reflect back on the times of learning in your life. How difficult was it for you to open your mind and heart to new truths? Did any of it involve a sense of loss or suffering?

_____

_____

_____

_____

2. How does learning more about Jesus enhance and/or sustain your faith?

_____

_____

_____

_____

3. What have been your new realities as you seek to know Jesus better?

_____

_____

_____

_____

> Lord Jesus, create within us a humble heart to accept what we yet need to learn. Forgive our overconfidence in our own knowledge and understanding. Give us the endurance to keep pursuing you into the place that you lead us. Let us always reflect the grace you bestow and the wisdom you impart.
>
> Amen.

121 Tuesday

Romans 15:17-21 (ERV)

I always want to tell the Good News in places where people have never heard of Christ. I do this because I don't want to build on the work that someone else has already started.

Reflection

As Paul winds down his letter, he makes a closing observation on his ministry efforts. Depending on the translation, Paul writes, "by word and deed…I have fulfilled the ministry of the gospel of Christ" (ESV). Or "by what I have said and done…I have fully proclaimed the gospel of Christ" (NIV). Once again, he intertwines the need for both explanation and demonstration. He doesn't merely tell people; he also shows them.

James, the brother of Jesus, urges this very spirit in his New Testament epistle. Using the metaphor of a mirror, he says that if we receive instruction from scripture but don't let it change what we think and do, it is like looking at our face in the mirror and then ignoring the reality of our broken selves staring back at us. Instead, we act as if nothing is wrong and nothing needs to change (James 1:23-25).

We cannot be content to merely launch scripture outward onto the world without also letting it go inward into us. As a disciple, we must be both speakers and doers of God's Word. This is not to suggest that our efforts earn us anything more than the grace Jesus has already given us. Nor does it mean we have to be perfect. Rather, it centers on the importance of authenticity. If we want to transform the world, let it begin with change in our own life.

Contemplation Questions

1. Assess your personal balance between "doing for Christ" and "being in Christ." Are they equally weighted or out of balance? What factors contribute to that?

_____
_____
_____
_____

2. How comfortable are you in making an honest assessment of your inward self? What are the barriers to doing that? How could you overcome them?

_____
_____
_____
_____

3. In your efforts to share Jesus with others, how authentic and consistent in what you say versus what you do?

_____
_____
_____
_____

> Heavenly Father, may your presence and your Word sink deep into the marrow of our bones. We remember that your words are not only the words of life, but life to the fullest. Forgive our wayward and inauthentic ways. Grant us pardon for all the times that our words were inconsistent with our actions. Restore us to our true identity. Guide us toward that which is genuine and life-changing.
>
> Amen.

122   Wednesday

Romans 15:22-29 (MSG)

And that's why it has taken me so long to finally get around to coming to you. But now that there is no more pioneering work to be done in these parts, and since I have looked forward to seeing you for many years, I'm planning my visit. I'm headed for Spain, and expect to stop off on the way to enjoy a good visit with you, and eventually have you send me off with God's blessing.

Reflection

Today's scripture is an example of how our plans can so easily go awry. Here, Paul plans his travel itinerary with a visit to Jerusalem, a stop in Rome, and then to proceed onward to present-day Spain, which at the time, was the western edge of civilization. The book of Acts tells us that he did eventually arrive in Rome, but not in the way he originally intended. He was arrested in Judea and then shipped to Rome where he spent two years under house arrest awaiting trial. Otherwise, scripture is silent on whether he made it to Spain.

Woody Allen is credited with the cliché, "If you want to make God laugh, tell him your plans." Apparently, it is based on an old Yiddish proverb, "We plan, God laughs." Or perhaps more explicitly from the book of James, "You who say, 'Today or tomorrow we will go to this or that city, spend a year there, carry on business and make money.' Why, you do not even know what will happen tomorrow. What is your life? You are a mist that appears for a little while and then vanishes. Instead, you ought to say, 'If it is the Lord's will, we will live and do this or that'" (James 4:13-15, NIV).

This is not to say we should never plan. Rather, we should seek to discern God's plan for us. This means we hold the ideas for our future gently and humbly. We temper our expectations, while developing skills of adaptability and flexibility. It is the spiritual discipline of looking forward without rushing ahead.

Contemplation Questions

1. On a scale of 1 to 10 (10 being highest), rate the importance you place on making plans for the future. How would you rate your response when those plans do not happen as you intended?

   _____

   _____

   _____

   _____

2. Assess your need for control. Are there specific areas in your life that you need more control? What are they? How does that need balance against allowing God to have control?

   _____

   _____

   _____

   _____

3. Describe how you discern God's plan for your future. Where do you look or who do you involve in that discernment? What might God be inviting you to do?

   _____

   _____

   _____

   _____

> Holy Spirit, forgive us our desire for ultimate control over our lives. We plan to our own ends but forget that you are the one who establishes our steps. May we turn to you for guidance. Give us peace to accept what is to come. Give us strength to follow you forward. Give us wisdom to discern your plan.
>
> Amen.

123   Thursday

Romans 15:30-33 (MSG)

I have one request, dear friends: Pray for me. Pray strenuously with and for me—to God the Father, through the power of our Master Jesus, through the love of the Spirit—that I will be delivered from the lions' den of unbelievers in Judea. Pray also that my relief offering to the Jerusalem believers will be accepted in the spirit in which it is given. Then, God willing, I'll be on my way to you with a light and eager heart, looking forward to being refreshed by your company. God's peace be with all of you. Oh, yes!

Reflection

The ancient Greek language is famous for having four different words that we translate into the single word "love" (they are: *storge*, *philia*, *eros*, and *agape*). So maybe it isn't surprising that the New Testament utilizes no less than six different Greek words for the word "prayer." Some are more commonly used than others. However, all illuminate a different approach and need.

The most common Greek word in scripture for prayer is *proseuchomai*. It is a compound word that communicates both form (facing toward) and substance (speaking aloud). While capturing all aspects of what we understand as prayer, it also suggests an aroma of worship. Sometimes *aiteo*, which literally means "ask," is translated as prayer when it carries with it an expectation of a response. Then there is *deomai*, which means to "beg" or "beseech." It carries with it a sense of urgency.

The simple reason behind multiple Greek words being used to express the single English word "prayer" is because it is an act of faith that is always contextual. In other words, not all prayers are the same any more than all "love" is the same. Our prayers can be directed in a multitude of directions and cover an infinite number of topics. The subject matter can be about us or can be offered on behalf of others. Prayers can be presented with quiet thanksgiving, demanded in anger, uttered in fear, or extended in humility. Indeed, it is a wonder that there aren't more words used to describe prayer.

Common to all these words and the contexts in which they denote is the foundational principle that we are able to communicate directly with the Lord through prayer. There is no need for filters, let alone an intermediary, for our connection to God. He is always present, listening, caring, and responsive to whatever we bring before him. Given God's posture toward our prayer, the challenge for us is why we don't do it more often.

Contemplation Questions

1. Assess and describe your "prayer life." Is it strong or weak? Is it frequent or intermittent? Do you do it solo or with others?

   _____
   _____
   _____
   _____

2. What do you notice about the subject matter of your prayers? How might you expand the scope of your prayers?

   _____
   _____
   _____
   _____

3. Have you ever "tracked" your prayers? In other words, have you paid attention to how God responded to your prayers? How would this help your prayer life?

   _____
   _____
   _____
   _____

Note on Prayer

Rather than me writing out a suggested prayer, I invite you to approach God the Father, Jesus the Son, and the Holy Spirit with your own words. Be bold. Be honest. Be willing. Be ready to connect to a divine that surpasses all understanding.

124 Friday

Romans 16:1-2 (MSG)

Be sure to welcome our friend Phoebe in the way of the Master, with all the generous hospitality we Christians are famous for. I heartily endorse both her and her work. She's a key representative of the church at Cenchrea. Help her out in whatever she asks. She deserves anything you can do for her. She's helped many a person, including me.

Reflection

As we enter the final chapter of Romans, Paul begins by mentioning a woman named Phoebe. This is the only time Phoebe is identified in the Bible, and so we have very little to know more about her. However, one clue we do get is that he identifies her with the Greek word *diakonos*, which literally translates as "servant" or "messenger." It is the root word for "deacon" or "deaconess." Interestingly, Paul identifies himself by the same title in his other letters.

All we do know for certain is that this woman gave help to Paul and many others in a newly founded church. She was faithful to what God put in front of her and served diligently and happily in the capacity and title granted to her by her home church. She used her life to make a significant difference in this world, and for God's kingdom.

Maybe our highest hope is that the same will be said of us in our specific giftedness in responding to the ministry opportunities God puts in front of us. While our name will not end up being mentioned in the Bible, we still can make a significant difference for God's kingdom and his glory.

Contemplation Questions

1. Imagine that God told you that your name would be mentioned in an enduring writing that would be read by millions of people over thousands of years. Would you live out your faith differently than you currently do? Why or why not?

   _____

   _____

   _____

   _____

2. What difference would it make to you if you knew the present and future impact of your faithfulness and service? What would you want to know?

   _____

   _____

   _____

   _____

3. How are you responding to the ministry invitation within your own church? Do you detect the difference you are making?

   _____

   _____

   _____

   _____

Heavenly Father, you give all of us the privilege of having an important role in your redeeming work here on earth. Forgive us when we shirk our responsibilities or try to deny others theirs. Forgive our overconfidence in our own knowledge and understanding. Give us the endurance to keep pursuing you into the place that you lead us. Let us always reflect the grace you bestow and the wisdom you impart.

Amen.

The Redeeming Road

125 — Saturday

Father, Son and Holy Spirit:

Forgive our wayward and inauthentic ways. We are overconfident in our own knowledge and understanding, and yet inconsistent in our own words and actions. We shirk our responsibilities and judge others in theirs.

Create within us a humble heart to accept what we yet need to learn. In our selfish desire for ultimate control over our lives, we quickly forget that you are the one who establishes our steps. We turn to you for guidance. Give us the endurance to keep pursuing you and the humility to accept your gentle leadership.

In relinquishing control, may we always reflect the grace you bestow and the wisdom you impart. May your presence and your word sink deep into the marrow of our bones, remembering that your words are not only the words of life, but life to the fullest. Then, and only then, we will be restored to our true identity.

Amen.

Week 18

Burgos, Spain

Week 19

Say hello to Priscilla and Aquila...
(MSG)

127 — Monday

Romans 16:3-5 (MSG)

Say hello to Priscilla and Aquila, who have worked hand in hand with me in serving Jesus. They once put their lives on the line for me. And I'm not the only one grateful to them. All the non-Jewish gatherings of believers also owe them plenty, to say nothing of the church that meets in their house.

Reflection

While taking a history exam during my seminary training, I was asked, "If I could meet any New Testament figure other than Jesus, who would it be?" My response was a toss-up between Eutychus, who fell asleep during one of Paul's long sermons (I feel ya, bro), and Priscilla and Aquila, a missionary couple who were closely allied to Paul. Although the facts surrounding them are still slim, their names show up seven different times in four different New Testament books, and always together as a pair.

Priscilla and Aquila are one of the rare instances in scripture where we find a couple working together as a ministry team. A notable example is their teaching of Apollos, who is thought to have gone on to be a highly effective evangelist. They were also very close friends with Paul and undoubtedly had an impact on him as they traveled together as fellow tentmakers. But they were always together, each with their own significance, but also interdependent and mutually supporting.

The reason I wanted to meet them is because I can identify with their story. I would love to compare notes with them to detect the parallel blessings in ministry life that I have been privileged to share with my own spouse. To see how the fullness of the story cannot be told without including both partners, a chance to celebrate the equal importance and substance of separate—and yet joined—contributions, and to recognize that this is another example of Jesus sending the disciples out in pairs, albeit with a slightly different angle.

Clearly, we can do ministry on our own. The New Testament is overflowing with examples of that reality. But we can also do it in partnership with a spouse, and neither approach is superior to the other. The important thing is to recognize that God can use all people and their relationships to further his story and reveal his glory.

Contemplation Questions

1. In general, how is God revealed in unique and different ways within a marriage?

   _____
   _____
   _____
   _____

2. How might that be carried over to a ministry shared by spouses?

   _____
   _____
   _____
   _____

3. If you are married, how might a shared ministry work for you both?

   _____
   _____
   _____
   _____

> Lord Jesus, thank you for the invitations to do ministry with and for you. But we also thank you for the option of doing that in partnership with our spouses. Whatever we bring, either singly or as a couple, we do so for your glory.
>
> Amen.

128

Tuesday

Romans 16:5-16 (MSG)

Hello to my dear friend Epenetus. He was the very first follower of Jesus in the province of Asia.

Hello to Mary. What a worker she has turned out to be!

Hello to my cousins Andronicus and Junias. We once shared a jail cell. They were believers in Christ before I was. Both of them are outstanding leaders.

Hello to Ampliatus, my good friend in the family of God.

Hello to Urbanus, our companion in Christ's work, and my good friend Stachys.

Hello to Apelles, a tried-and-true veteran in following Christ.

Hello to the family of Aristobulus.

Hello to my cousin Herodion.

Hello to those who belong to the Lord from the family of Narcissus.

Hello to Tryphena and Tryphosa—such diligent women in serving the Master.

Hello to Persis, a dear friend and hard worker in Christ.

Hello to Rufus—a good choice by the Master!—and his mother. She has also been a dear mother to me.

Hello to Asyncritus, Phlegon, Hermes, Patrobas, Hermas, and also to all of their families.

Hello to Philologus, Julia, Nereus and his sister, and Olympas—and all the followers of Jesus who live with them.

Holy hugs all around! All the churches of Christ send their warmest greetings!

Reflection

When a Hollywood movie reaches its conclusion, the end is marked by the closing credits scrolling over the screen. It is our cue to get up and leave, mostly because the names and titles mean nothing to us. Here in Chapter 16, Paul provides essentially the same thing, and true to form, we have the same reaction as we do at the end of a movie. Our eyes gloss over and we speed-read through.

But consider that Paul put these names in here not because he *had* to, but because he *wanted* to. Moreover, those names teach us something important. Much like movie credits identify everyone who was involved in making the movie–from the big ideas right down to the seemingly unimportant details–everyone had a role to fulfill. Paul–through his litany of names–is telling us the same thing. All these people had a role in his life and in his ministry. Big and small. Each is important. The book of Romans is not the same without every one of them.

We know Scripture is written in a way so that it always reveals God. Specifically, scripture reveals God in the best way we know God– through his Son Jesus. But God also reveals himself in other ways. In nature. In miracles. In answered prayer. And perhaps most commonly in us. We are living scripture; it just so happens we are not in the canon.

I often wonder if we saw our names listed in scripture, would our attitude and outlook change? Would we see ourselves differently? Would we conduct ourselves better? Would we be attentive to the legacy we would leave behind? But just because our names and stories aren't in the Bible, doesn't mean they are unimportant. Just because they are not recorded here, doesn't mean they are not noticed. Our heavenly Father sees all–knows all–remembers all. He, along with Jesus, and all the heavenly hosts, is watching, cheering, encouraging, and working with us toward ultimate wins.

They are telling us to write our story–

Write a *good* story.

Write an *encouraging* story.

Write a story that is *worthy* of being in scripture.

It can be big. It can be small. But all of it contributes to God's beautiful story.

Contemplation Questions

1. The people we encounter in the Bible had no idea their names and stories would end up in scripture. Do you think they would have conducted themselves differently had they known? Why?

_____

_____

_____

_____

2. Imagine you had an extended encounter with a person who was specifically mentioned in scripture. Would that change how you accepted what they said or offered? If so, how and why?

_____

_____

_____

_____

3. In what ways has God revealed himself through others to you?

_____

_____

_____

_____

> Heavenly Father, we are your children, but we are also witnesses to the world of your love, grace, and redemption. Forgive us when we neglect that privilege. Remind us of your identity. Encourage us in our testimony. Restore us to the kingdom tasks you have placed in front of us. Lead us in the way we should go.
>
> Amen.

129 — Wednesday

Romans 16:17-18 (MSG)

One final word of counsel, friends. Keep a sharp eye out for those who take bits and pieces of the teaching that you learned and then use them to make trouble. Give these people a wide berth. They have no intention of living for our Master Christ. They're only in this for what they can get out of it, and aren't above using pious sweet talk to dupe unsuspecting innocents.

Reflection

Troublemakers. Agitators. Dissenters. At first glance, we would consider all these descriptions with negative connotations. Unless, of course, we are one of them and view our position as the just cause or following the right path. Then we see ourselves as advocates, truth-speakers, or patriots. Which descriptor to apply depends on one's perspective.

When it comes to people who teach faith, Paul gives discerning direction on how to tell one from another. He says the determining factor is whether the person is acting in service of Jesus. Often that can be a tough call for us to make, especially when the person Paul is warning us about is gifted with "good words and fair speeches" (KJV). Instead, we are urged to look past the smooth talk and flashy presentation to see if the person's actions and life are in alignment with what Jesus taught. Is there consistency between word and deed?

When I am making that evaluation of a faith teacher's trustworthiness, the key characteristic I look for is peaceful presence. Do they lean more toward grace instead of judgment? Are they more interested in dwelling with the people instead of spreading the "correct" theology? (Full disclosure: I fall short of that standard more than I like to admit.) James, the brother of Jesus, gives a good measuring stick, "For judgment is without mercy to one who has shown no mercy. Mercy triumphs over judgment" (James 2:13). As such, the marks of a good teacher bends toward forgiveness, pursues restoration, and always looks for God's redemption.

Contemplation Questions

1. Describe the qualities or characteristics you look for in a "good teacher" to help you grow in your faith. How would you characterize the spiritual/faith teachers you currently have in your life? Does your response to the first question align with your response to the second question?

___

___

___

___

2. Think of a time when you have taught or guided someone else. What qualities or characteristics would that person say you possess?

___

___

___

___

3. Describe how you are mindfully developing or enhancing your teaching/leading qualities and characteristics. What are you satisfied with? What needs more attention?

___

___

___

___

> Jesus, we experience our gifts through the unity of the body that calls us to set aside divisiveness. We pray and celebrate together. We speak encouragement and expect accountability. We practice active listening, careful discernment, and personal attentiveness, both in our lives and the ministry you set before us. Through the Spirit, give us wisdom and discernment. May you lead us to speak truth and practice mercy.
>
> Amen.

130 — Thursday

Romans 16:19-20 (ERV)

The God who brings peace will soon defeat Satan and give you power over him. The grace of our Lord Jesus be with you.

Reflection

There is an old saying in the military: "There are no atheists in a foxhole." It means that everyone believes in a higher power when the possibility of a sudden and violent death is both very real and very close. I remember encountering this adage for the first time during my Army days. Oddly enough, I was a definite atheist back then, but because I never served in a combat zone, the truth of the saying was never put to the test.

Now that I am a Christian, I would add this addendum to the adage: "A foxhole is the last place you want to figure out how to pray." In other words, being caught up in situations of severe stress and conflict is overwhelming enough without having to learn how to connect to God in the midst of it. For sure, God is always present, willing, and available to us no matter our circumstance, but the potential obstacle lies on our end of the equation. Do we really want to be searching for a connection with him while our world explodes all around us? And have we developed enough in our own discipleship to set aside fear, anxiety, and confusion to make full use of that connection?

In our scripture passage, Paul is commending his readers for having taken steps of preparation. He reassures them, and us, that God will crush Satan and bring ultimate victory in his own timing. But until then, he urges them and us "to be wise in doing right and to stay innocent of any wrong" (Romans 16:19, NLT). He is advocating for learning how to pray before having a dire need to pray. He wants us to expand our connection with God before being pressed to connect to God. Being "prepared" is nothing more than pursuing the life of a disciple before it is put to the test.

Contemplation Questions

1. How does your prayer life inform the rest of your life? Can you make straight line connections between the two?

   _____

   _____

   _____

   _____

2. Describe your typical manner of praying. Are you open to different methods of prayer? Might a different method enhance your experience with God? Why or why not?

   _____

   _____

   _____

   _____

3. We easily see the value of prayer from our side of the relationship with God. What might be the value God experiences when we are intentional and faithful in our prayer life?

   _____

   _____

   _____

   _____

Lord Jesus, forgive us when we neglect or ignore our connection to you as well as for all the times we ignore the invitation of prayer or the discipline of study. Remind us that we are not on our own. We belong to you, and you prize the relationship we enjoy. Lead us in the ways where we can feel encouragement and experience strengthening in our connection. Guide us into your presence as we approach the end of this week.

Amen.

131   Friday

Romans 16:21-24 (MSG)

And here are some more greetings from our end. Timothy, my partner in this work, Lucius, and my cousins Jason and Sosipater all said to tell you hello.

   I, Tertius, who wrote this letter at Paul's dictation, send you my personal greetings.

   Gaius, who is host here to both me and the whole church, wants to be remembered to you.

   Erastus, the city treasurer, and our good friend Quartus send their greetings.

Reflection

Here we get a "peek behind the curtain" to Paul's ministry—the people in his everyday life that supported and partnered with him in carrying out God's mission. We learn that Paul didn't physically write the book of Romans but dictated it. It was Tertius who actually put pen to paper. He used his training and skills to keep the wisdom and instruction of God, by the Holy Spirit and through Paul, from immediately disappearing into the ether the moment they were spoken.

But it didn't end there. There were countless scribes in the tradition of Tertius who made copies of this letter and all the other books of the New Testament. Before the advent of the printing press fourteen centuries later, this is how the Word of God was preserved and shared. But unlike Tertius, we don't know their names. We only know their faithful work.

We will dive deeper into this theme in our final devotional entry. For today, consider your contributions to the preservation and sharing of God's Word. As Paul challenged us back in Chapter 10: How can anyone call on God unless they believe? And how can they believe if they have never heard? And how can they hear unless someone tells them? And how will anyone tell them without being sent? How beautiful the feet of the one who brings good news.

Contemplation Questions

1. Reflect on your faith journey as it stands today. Is it easy or difficult for you to detect your contributions to God's Kingdom? Why?

___

___

___

___

2. In God's Kingdom, some are called to actively lead, while others are called to serve as a support. How might God be asking you to lead like Paul? How might you be invited to serve in a role that is similar to Tertius?

___

___

___

___

3. Imagine some of the ways God will reveal himself in your efforts of leading and/or serving.

___

___

___

___

> Father in heaven, we give honor and glory to your name. Not only have you delivered us from death, you call us into service for your kingdom's sake. We have the privilege to trumpet your love, announce your grace, and share about your redemption. Encourage and guide us in its use. May we never neglect it or take it for granted.
>
> Amen.

The Redeeming Road

132 — Saturday

Holy Father, Lord Jesus, and Holy Spirit:

Forgive us for when we neglect or ignore our connection to you. We neglect the privilege you have extended to us when we ignore the invitation of prayer or fail to engage in the discipline of study. You invite us into light, but we choose to stay in darkness.

Remind us that we are not on our own, but belong to you—body, mind, and soul. Our very identity is found in you. Lead us in the ways where we can feel encouragement and experience strengthening in our connection. As an expression of the unity of your body that is found in all of us, we pray and celebrate together. We speak encouragement and expect accountability. We practice active listening, careful discernment, and personal attentiveness, both in our lives and the ministry you set before us.

Give us wisdom and discernment. Lead us to speak truth and practice mercy. Restore us to the kingdom tasks you have placed in front of us. May we be witnesses to the world of your love, grace, and redemption.

Amen.

Week 19

Burgos, Spain

Closing Devotional

All of our praise rises to the One who is strong enough to make you strong...
(MSG)

134

Romans 16:25-27 (MSG)

All of our praise rises to the One who is strong enough to make *you* strong, exactly as preached in Jesus Christ, precisely as revealed in the mystery kept secret for so long but now an open book through the prophetic Scriptures. All the nations of the world can now know the truth and be brought into obedient belief, carrying out the orders of God, who got all this started, down to the final detail.

All our praise is focused through Jesus on this incomparably wise God! Yes!

Reflection

In the Nativity story, I love that it was shepherds who first received the news of Jesus' birth. For generations, Jerusalem and all of Judea had been waiting for a conquering warrior king, a superhero to overthrow the occupying armies. They also expected the highest echelons of society would be the first to know. But when the savior king did arrive, the angels picked lowly field hands as the audience to first receive the news. If we spend any time in the scriptures, we recognize how God values humility and his preference for associating with the "lowly." This is how God rolls.

It would be fair to view Paul from the same perspective. Yes, he is responsible for authoring the majority of the New Testament, and his words have shaped our theology more than any other source outside of Jesus. But at the time, no one would have predicted he was destined to be God's scribe. Certainly, God prepared him throughout his life for this eventual role, but no one foresaw that it would turn out the way that it did—perhaps Paul least of all.

That surprising outcome shaped Paul's understanding of God. If he has given us anything in Romans, it is his repeated emphasis on the importance of faith. He employs the word "faith" more in the book of Romans than any other letter he wrote. He teaches us that faith is not based on sight, but upon dependence and perseverance in God. He reminds us that we are saved by faith, so we must stand and live by faith. We must strengthen and encourage each other's faith. In fact, faith is the last word he uses before the closing salutation of the book. For Paul, faith is the engine that drives everything else.

As we read these final words of the book of Romans, we must always remember to take up the challenge of faith. Too often we tell ourselves that we are not worthy, prepared, or chosen for a significant role within God's unfolding kingdom. We forget the story of the shepherds of the Nativity and ignore the events of Paul's life. We are too quick to fold our tents and depart the harvest field before we have given God the chance to develop us into the fullness of who he created us to be, and the role he has given us to fulfill. In short, we must always…Keep the Faith.

Contemplation Questions

1. Can you describe your significance to God? Do you recognize that your identity in God is above and beyond what you are able to contribute to God's Kingdom?

___

2. How are you encouraged with the realization that God prefers to move and work with the humble and lowly? What does that say about God? What does that say about you?

___

3. What steps can you take to explore and realize the fullness of who God created you to be?

___

> Lord God, thank you for leading us on this journey through your Word. Bless us with its grace. Reassure us with its truth. Guide us with its wisdom. Strengthen us so we can always adhere to the faith you have instilled in us.
>
> Amen.

A Closing Blessing

We have reached the end of *The Redeeming Road*. Our journey together has covered twenty weeks. I hope you have found the trip to be challenging, enlightening, uplifting, and maybe at times, exhilarating. I have found it to be so, especially on those days when I didn't feel like writing. Invariably, the Holy Spirit always convinced me to engage, provided me with the words to share, and gave me the stamina to get them written. May you find the same motivation and strength each day, and your discipleship process vibrant and moving forward. Thank you for your participation, your encouragement, and your patience while walking the road together.

From the Author

I did not grow up in a Christian home, nor enjoy the benefits of a church community. Indeed, most of my first three decades on this planet were decidedly apathetic toward anything dealing with God, faith, or spirituality. I saw life as a race, and the prize for running it well was anything that fed my self-absorbed ego. Indeed, in a perverse way, my upbringing *did* teach me to know a god, to love a god, and to worship a god…so long as the god's name was Art DeBruyn.

The pivotal change happened when Jesus finally barged into my life to such a degree that I could no longer avoid the reality of his existence. I told my story and was baptized on March 16, 1997 at the age of 36. At the time, I really didn't anticipate my life to change as much as it has. Within the short span of four years, I left my profession as a trial attorney to become a youth pastor, and one year later, enrolled in seminary. Even then, I never envisioned that he would then call me to serve in the capacity of a lead pastor of two different churches. It only confirms the truth that Jesus accepts us where he finds us, but he doesn't leave us there.

In the process, I have discovered that attending to my faith supplies nourishment, acting with virtue and integrity provides shelter, searching for wisdom brings light, and above all, seeking the Lord in everything I do gives protection. This devotional is my contribution toward helping all travelers of faith undertake the daily steps of the journey.

A.B. "Art" DeBruyn

A.B. "Art" DeBruyn was born to immigrant parents from Europe and grew up in Grand Rapids, Michigan. After serving in the United States Army as a military policeman, he graduated from Michigan State University and Southern Illinois University School of Law. He practiced civil litigation for a decade before entering Western Theological Seminary. After graduating, he has served as lead pastor for churches in Boulder, Colorado, and Indianapolis, Indiana. Married to Christy for 35 years, they enjoy spending time with their three adult daughters and their spouses. He can be reached at his website, 221.life.

www.ingramcontent.com/pod-product-compliance
Lightning Source LLC
Chambersburg PA
CBHW060458010526
44118CB00018B/2454